DEC 0 2 1991			
DEC 1 6 1996			
MAY 2 9 2007			
JAN 0 5 2009			
	261-2500		Printed in USA

ENTERED AUG 2 8 1991

RECRUITING, INTERVIEWING, SELECTING, AND ORIENTING NEW EMPLOYEES

Diane Arthur

amacom
AMERICAN MANAGEMENT ASSOCIATION

Library of Congress Cataloging-in-Publication Data

Arthur, Diane.
    Recruiting, interviewing, selecting, and orienting
new employees.

    Includes index.
    1. Recruiting of employees.   2. Employment
interviewing.   3. Employee selection.   I. Title.
II. Title: Orienting new employees.
HF5549.5.R44A75   1986   658.3'11   85–48216
ISBN 0-8144-5539-5

To
Warren, my foundation,
and
Valerie, my inspiration

PREFACE

This book is designed to serve as a guide for anyone involved in the recruitment, interviewing, selection, or orientation steps of the employment process. For those who are not human resource development specialists, it will provide the skills, tools, and techniques needed to operate effectively in these areas. (The terms *human resource development specialists* and *personnel specialists* will be used interchangeably throughout this book. Although the trend has been toward the more all-encompassing term human resources, many organizations still refer to this field as personnel.) Depending on a variety of factors, including the size of an organization and the role of human resource experts within that organization, senior executives, managers, and supervisors often find themselves performing personnel functions fairly regularly. Because so few professionals perceive personnel-related tasks to be an integral part of their job, they may approach this area of responsibility with some trepidation. The increased impact of equal employment opportunity and affirmative action laws and regulations on the hiring process can also be unnerving to those who are unfamiliar with this aspect of the employment process.

This book will guide those human resource development professionals who are new to the field and need step-by-step guidance. It will be a useful refresher for those who have worked in the field for some time and wish to update or upgrade their skills. It may also serve as a basic reference for training workshops in various aspects of the employment process.

The book has been written in logical, sequential order, following the steps which normally occur in the hiring process. Therefore, I recommend that it be read chapter by chapter.

The methods and techniques described in this book are applicable to all work environments: corporate and nonprofit; union and nonunion; technical and nontechnical; large and small. They may be applied to both professional and nonprofessional positions. Readers are advised to consider the particulars of their own company and apply the concepts discussed here accordingly.

Recruiting, interviewing, hiring, and orienting new employees are specific skills. How well you practice these skills can directly affect many common organizational problem areas, such as turnover, employee morale, and absenteeism. By carefully practicing and implementing the methods described in this book, any organization can greatly improve its employer-employee relations and its level of productivity.

CONTENTS

1

Familiarization with the Details of a Job

There are a number of steps in the employment process that must be accomplished before sitting down with a candidate for a face-to-face interview. Even before applications for a specific opening are solicited and the recruitment process begins, there is a great deal of preparation to be done.

The very first preparatory step to be taken is familiarization with the details of a job. This important step will provide necessary answers to four key questions.

1. Am I thoroughly familiar with the qualities being sought in an applicant?
2. Are these qualities both job-related and realistic?
3. Can I clearly communicate the duties and responsibilities of this position to the applicants?
4. Am I prepared to provide additional relevant information about the job and the company to the applicants?

DUTIES AND RESPONSIBILITIES

The job-familiarization process begins with a review of the specific duties and responsibilities of the position. If you are a human resource specialist, make it a point to spend time in the department where the opening exists. Observe and converse with the incumbent as he or she performs various aspects of the job. Talk to the supervisor in charge for his or her perspective of the scope of work involved. If possible, seek out people who have previously held the position to see how the job may have evolved. Try to visit on more than one occasion so that you will be able to observe a typical day.

If a personal visit is not possible, have lengthy telephone conversations with several departmental representatives. Also request a job description and review its contents for a detailed description of the level and degree of responsibility. Job descriptions are an interviewer's most valuable tool. There are guidelines for developing maximally effective job descriptions at the end of this chapter.

It is extremely important for personnel specialists to learn as much as possible about the responsibilities of a given job. Not only will it prepare them for the face-to-face interview, but it will also help to establish a rapport between the personnel staff and a specific department. This is critical, since in many organizations there is some dispute as to who should recruit, interview, and select new employees: human resource development experts or department heads and other specialists in a given field. The argument against personnel grows stronger if the position in question is highly technical in nature, since personnel representatives are usually not technically trained. This is a difficult argument to resolve. On the one hand, it is quite true that human resource experts do not have the in-depth knowledge of a particular job that someone in the field possesses. On the other hand, they have a wide range of overall interviewing skills, which enable them to ascertain the information needed to make appropriate hiring decisions.

The ideal arrangement is a partnership between the human resource department and the department in which an opening exists. The personnel specialist should screen the resumes and applications, and conduct the initial interview to determine overall job suitability. Referrals may then be made to the other department, where a more detailed, technical interview can be held. As a final step, representatives from both departments should compare notes and reach a joint final decision.

Human resource development specialists are cautioned not to consider themselves experts in a field other than their own simply because they learn certain jargon. If such expertise is assumed, one of two things is likely to occur: you will be convincing enough so that the applicant believes you know more than you really do and proceeds to ask technical questions beyond your realm of knowledge; or the applicant will see through your facade, particularly if key terms are misused. In either instance, the results are unnecessarily embarrassing.

Human resource experts are urged to learn as much as possible about the specific jobs they are trying to fill, but should always concentrate on their personnel skills first and foremost.

Department heads and other departmental representatives should also thoroughly familiarize themselves with the degree and level of responsibility required for a given job. It is dangerous to assume that technical know-how and work experience within the department in which an opening exists automatically impart knowledge of the specific duties of that job. It is especially important that departmental representatives step back and objectively evaluate its scope. Are the required tasks realistic in relation to other factors, such as previous experience and education? Are they relevant to the overall job function? Do they overlap with the responsibilities of another job?

One final comment needs to be made about familiarization with the duties of a job. This process should take place *each time* that a position becomes available. Even if a position was filled six months ago and is now vacant again, the responsibilities of the job should be assessed to make certain that no major changes have occurred in the interim. This will ensure up-to-date job information and accuracy when discussing the position with potential employees.

EDUCATION AND PRIOR EXPERIENCE

The next step in the familiarization process concerns the role of educational credentials and prior work experience. Equal employment opportunity legislation must be considered in conjunction with these areas and will be examined more closely in Chapter 4. For now, consider the following questions when trying to determine the appropriateness of educational and experiential job requirements.

1. What kind of prior experience and education is necessary to perform the essential functions of this job successfully?
2. Could someone without this experience or education handle the job?
3. If the answer to question 2 is no, ask why not. What is it about this job that dictates a certain level of education or a certain number of years of work experience?

Arbitrarily setting high minimum standards in the hope of filling a position with the most qualified person possible can backfire. For example, suppose that you are trying to fill a first-line supervisor's slot and you decide that you want someone who not only has a great deal of hands-on experience, but who is also well-rounded. To you, this translates into someone with at least five years of supervisory experience and a four-year college degree. If you asked yourself the three questions just suggested, you would probably conclude that these requirements are too high for a first-line supervisory position. Also, for reasons of equal employment opportunity you would have to modify them. Even if there were no applicable employment laws however, there is a good reason for setting more flexible standards: if you came across applicants who fell short of your experience and education profile, but who met other intangible or nonconcrete requirements and came highly recommended, you would not be able to hire them. It would be difficult to justify hiring someone who did not meet the minimum requirements of the job, especially if you also rejected candidates who exceeded them.

In addition to asking yourself the three basic questions regarding experience and education, there is a way of setting requirements that does not paint you into a corner, but still allows you to be highly selective. By using carefully worded terminology in the job description, you can allow yourself room to choose the candidate who best combines concrete and intangible requirements. These phrases include:

Extensive experience required
In-depth knowledge of _____ required
Degree highly desirable

Degree preferred
An equivalent combination of education and experience

These sample phrases all provide the latitude to select someone who, for example, may be lacking in one area, such as education, but who compensates with a great deal of experience. The use of such terms does not mean that hiring standards are compromised; rather, it means that care is being taken to avoid setting requirements that cannot be justified by the specific duties of the job, while at the same time offering the widest possible range of choice among applicants.

INTANGIBLE REQUIREMENTS

In the previous section reference was made to intangible criteria and how they can help balance the lack of specific educational or experiential requirements. Intangible factors might include:

Management style
Ability to get along with co-workers, management and
   subordinates
Initiative
Creativity and imagination
Self-confidence
Personality
Temperament
Responsiveness
Appearance
Maturity

When becoming familiar with the details of a job, it is a good idea to explore the question of what type of individual would be most compatible with the position. This can best be determined by learning as much as possible about the required duties, the level and degree of responsibility, the amount of stress involved, the amount of independent work as opposed to work that is closely supervised, and the overall management style of the department. Keeping this ideal employee profile in mind as candidates are considered can be helpful, particularly if there are two or more applicants who similarly meet the concrete requirements of the job. You can then compare intangible job-related factors in making the final decision. However, be careful not to weigh intangible elements too heavily. They are highly subjective, and selecting someone solely on the basis of one of these factors is not recommended. If considered at all, such factors must be job related.

REPORTING RELATIONSHIPS AND DECISION MAKING

Another facet of the familiarization process has to do with reporting relationships. In this regard, the following questions should be asked.

1. What position will this job report to, both directly and indirectly?
2. Where does this job appear on the department's organizational chart?
3. What positions, if any, report directly and/or indirectly to this job?
4. What is the relationship between this job and other jobs in the department, in terms of level and scope of responsibility?
5. What is the relationship between this job and other jobs in the organization?

It is important to note that all these questions pertain to *positions*, as opposed to specific individuals. This eliminates the possibility of the answers being influenced by the personality or skill of a particular employee.

In addition to understanding reporting relationships, an understanding of the department's decision-making process is important to interviewers for two reasons: it gives them a more complete picture of the available position and prepares them to answer questions that applicants are likely to ask. Consider which positions in the department are responsible for decisions regarding:

Salary increases
Promotions
Performance appraisals
Transfers
Disciplinary actions
Vacations
Leaves of absence

By being prepared with this information, you will be better able to describe the full scope of the decision-making responsibilities of the available position.

WORK ENVIRONMENT

The next aspect of familiarization with a position concerns the work environment. In this regard, four different factors should be considered.

1. The first has to do with physical working conditions. This encompasses such factors as sitting or standing for long periods of time; working in areas that may not be well ventilated; exposure to chemicals or toxic fumes; working in cramped quarters; and working in a very noisy location. If the working conditions are ideal, few interviewers will hesitate to inform prospective employees of this. After all, this helps to sell the company and the job, and might even make up for areas that are less ideal—perhaps the starting salary is not up to par with that of a competitor, or the benefits package is not as comprehensive. However, if the working conditions leave something to be desired, the tendency is to omit reference to them when discussing the job. This is done in the hope that once an employee begins work and discovers the flaw in the work environment he or she will adjust, rather than leave. Unfortunately, what frequently occurs is that a new employee re-

sents the deception and either quits or develops a negative attitude.

The problems of high turnover and low morale as they relate to unsatisfactory working conditions can easily be prevented. In order to do this you must first accurately describe existing working conditions to prospective employees. If an unpleasant condition is temporary, by all means say so, but do not make anything up. Be sure to ask candidates whether they have ever worked under similar conditions before and for how long. Also determine how they feel about being asked to work under these circumstances. When they respond to your questions, it is as important to watch as it is to listen to their answers. Often there is a contradiction between an applicant's verbal and nonverbal response. Your skill as an interviewer will in part be determined by how well you incorporate and evaluate each type of response to reach a decision. Chapter 5 will deal with the issues of active listening and nonverbal communication more fully. For now, suffice it to say that if a candidate states that he does not mind standing eight hours a day, but you sense some resistance from his body language, you must pursue the subject until you are more certain of his true reaction.

Another accurate way to assess a potential employee's response to uncomfortable working conditions is to actually show the person where he or she would be working. Unless this is logistically impractical, a quick trip to the job site should be part of the interview. This way there are no surprises and a new employee knows exactly what to expect when reporting to work for the first time.

2. A second aspect of the work environment with which an interviewer should be familiar is the geographic location of the job. As was already stated, if at all possible it is a good idea to show potential employees where they would be working. If recruiting from a central office for positions in satellite branches, be specific in the description of the job site. If pamphlets or brochures are available illustrating the location where an opening exists, offer them to the applicant.

Occasionally, interviewers will not know exactly where a new employee will be assigned. For example, approval may have been obtained to hire a half-dozen security guards for different branches of a bank, but at the time of recruitment it may not be clear which branches the guards are to be assigned to. In this instance, describe all the possible locations and ask applicants for their preferences. Be certain to ask whether there are any branches where they would definitely not want to be assigned, and make a note of this. Do not make the mistake of assuming that someone will not want to work at a specific location because you deem it to be a lengthy or inconvenient commute. Likewise, it is unwise to assume that someone will find a certain site desirable just because it is close to his or her home. In other words, do not decide for yourself what the applicant wants.

Sometimes a position will call for rotation from one location to another. If this is the case, be prepared to describe the working conditions of each location and how long each assignment is likely to last. Be sure to solicit a reaction to the idea of job rotation. Many employees like to get settled into a work routine where they are familiar with the environment, the commute, and the other workers. On the other hand, some people like the variety offered by a rotational position.

3. Related to location is the issue of travel. Obviously, if it is known that a job requires traveling, this must be communicated to a prospective employee. Be sure to discuss the geographic span and the expected frequency of job-related travel. In the case of local travel applicants will want to know whether they will be expected to provide their own means of transportation or whether a company car is to be provided. If the employee is to use his or her own car, how is reimbursement for mileage and any required maintenance handled? For long-distance trips, including those abroad, it is important to know how related expenses are to be reimbursed.

Often, a job does not currently require travel, but is expected to in the near future. This fact should be conveyed to applicants. Try to be as specific as possible, even though you cannot say exactly how much traveling is involved or where it will be done. Perhaps you can identify a percentage of work time that the employee can expect to spend traveling—say between 10 and 25 percent—and a general locale—such as the New England states.

4. Another element of a work environment with which an interviewer should be familiar is the specific schedule. This is

especially important for clerical and entry-level positions, where employees expect to be told when to report to work each day and when they may leave. Although executives, managers, and supervisors generally assume that they will come in early and work late as required, they too need to know what the standard hours are. Many companies utilize flex-time, whereby all workers are on the job during specific core hours, but then vary in their starting and quitting times. Hence, jobs are not necessarily on a traditional nine to five schedule.

Organizations also vary in the practice of how long a workweek is, generally ranging from 35 to 40 hours. For an employee who must attend a class beginning at 6:00 P.M., leaving work at 5:15 P.M. instead of 5:00 P.M. could make a big difference.

Also be sure to know how much time is allotted for meals, as well as other scheduled breaks throughout the day. Conveying this information to applicants can prevent future disciplinary problems after they become employees.

Finally, when learning about a job schedule do not omit the days of the week to be worked. Not all departments are on a Monday through Friday schedule. The job may require working alternate weekends or evenings. If this is the case, find out how days off are scheduled.

EXEMPTION STATUS

Another facet of a job to be familiar with is its exemption status. As defined by the Fair Labor Standards Act, the term *exempt* literally means exempt from overtime compensation—an employer is not required to pay exempt employees for time worked beyond their regularly scheduled workweek. This generally pertains to executives, managers, and supervisors. As mentioned earlier, individuals who fall into these categories assume that they will occasionally be required to put in extra hours without receiving compensation. The term *nonexempt* literally means not exempt from overtime compensation. Nonexempt employees, such as clerical workers, must be paid for all additional hours worked.

With most positions there is no question as to their exemption status. However, some jobs fall into a grey area and are not as easily categorized. Whether employees are exempt or nonexempt depends on their duties and responsibilities, as well as on their salaries. To avoid errors in classification, you can obtain guidelines from the U.S. Department of Labor, Employment Standards Administration, Wage and Hour Division, Washington, D.C. 20210.

SALARY RANGES

The next aspect of familiarization with a position concerns salary ranges. Whether or not this information is disclosed to an applicant at the initial interview is a matter of company policy, but the interviewer should certainly know what a job will pay so that he or she can determine whether further consideration of a candidate is warranted. If, for example, there is an opening for an administrative assistant paying from $18,500 to $25,500 per year and an applicant is currently earning an annual salary of $20,000 there is no problem. If, on the other hand, a supervisory position becomes available offering a salary range of from $26,000 to $37,500 and an applicant is currently making $37,000, there are a number of areas to be concerned about. What is your company's policy regarding starting a new employee at the maximum of his or her salary range? If you offer the maximum, will this person want to accept an increase of just $500 a year? What about subsequent salary increases? Will he or she be "red circled" for being at the ceiling of the range and therefore, remain frozen at $37,500 until either the salary structure is reevaluated or the position is reclassified?

Having this kind of salary-related information before interviewing can help save time for both the interviewer and the applicant.

UNION STATUS

Interviewers should also be familiar with the union status of a job. Be prepared to tell applicants whether or not they will be required to join a union, which union it is, how much the dues are, and what being a union member essentially entails. Exercise caution when discussing this topic and do not disclose personal views. Your statements on this subject should be restricted to objective description and information.

GROWTH OPPORTUNITIES

Another aspect of the familiarization process has to do with growth opportunities. Most people are interested in knowing whether they will be able to move up in an organization. In this regard it is helpful for the interviewer to have the following information.

> Policies regarding promotions
> Frequency of salary reviews and increases
> Relationship of a position's level and scope of responsibility to that of others within a job family (for example, the duties of a junior accountant compared with those of an accountant or senior accountant)
> Policies governing internal job posting
> Likelihood of advancement

Even if an applicant does not ask about growth opportunities, interviewers can volunteer the information as a means of making the company more attractive to prospective employees.

SPECIAL REQUIREMENTS

Finally, interviewers need to consider any special requirements of the job. An example of this might be the wearing of a uniform. Applicants will want to know whether or not the company provides the uniform, who pays for the cost of cleaning and replacement, and whether lockers are provided.

JOB DESCRIPTIONS

At first glance, familiarization with the details of a job may seem like an overwhelming task. However, there is a single tool that can consolidate the steps and provide all the information needed. That tool is a job description—a formalized document of factual and concise information descriptive of the identity of the job, its responsibilities and the work it entails. This multipurpose tool can be used in virtually every aspect of the employment process. Here are some of its uses.

Recruitment
Interviewing
Selection
Job posting
Manpower planning
Training and development
Performance appraisal
Promotion
Transfer
Disciplinary action
Demotions
Grievance proceedings
Employee orientation
Work flow analysis
Salary administration structuring
Clarifying relationships between jobs and work assignments
Surveys and job pricing
Exit interviews

Since job descriptions can be used for so many different purposes, care should be taken to write them as comprehensively as possible. Initially, this will require a fair amount of time, but it will be well worth the effort.

Here are some guidelines for how to go about writing a job description.

1. *Arrange duties and responsibilities in a logical, sequential*

order. Begin with the task requiring the greatest amount of time or carrying the greatest responsibility.

2. *State separate duties clearly and concisely.* This way anyone can glance at the description and easily identify each duty.

3. *Try to avoid generalizations or ambiguous words.* Use specific language and be exact in your meaning. To illustrate: "handles mail" might be better expressed as "sorts mail" or "distributes mail."

4. *Do not try to list every task.* Use the phrase "primary duties and responsibilities include . . ." at the beginning of your job description and proceed from there. You may also choose to close with the phrase, "performs other related duties and responsibilities, as required."

5. *Include specific examples of duties wherever possible.*

6. *Use nontechnical language.* A good job description explains the responsibilities of a job in terms that are understandable to everyone using it.

7. *Indicate the frequency of occurrence of each duty.* One popular way of doing this is to have a column on the left of the list of tasks with corresponding percentages that represent the estimated amount of time devoted to each primary duty.

8. *List duties individually and concisely, rather than using narrative paragraph form*; a job description is not an English composition.

9. *Do not refer to specific people.* Instead refer to titles and positions. Incumbents are likely to change positions long before the positions themselves are revamped or eliminated.

10. *Use the present tense*; it reads more smoothly.

11. *Be objective and accurate in describing the job.* Be careful not to describe the present incumbent, yourself when you held that particular job, someone who may have just been fired for poor performance, or someone who was recently promoted for outstanding job performance. Describe the job as it should be performed—not as you would like to see it performed.

12. *Stress what the incumbent does, instead of attempting to explain a procedure that must be used.* To illustrate, use *records appointments* rather than *a record of appointments must be kept.*

13. *Be certain that all requirements are job-related and are in accordance with equal employment opportunity laws and regulations.*

14. *Eliminate unnecessary articles,* such as *a* and *the.* Do not

make the description too wordy. Most job descriptions can be completed in one or two pages. The length of a job description does not increase the importance of the job.

15. *Use action words.* This means any word that describes a specific function, such as *organizes*. Action words do not leave room for confusion. Within a sentence one word should stand out as most descriptive; a word that could really stand alone. This action word will also convey to the reader a degree of responsibility. For example, compare *directs* to *under the direction of*. . . . Try to begin each sentence with an action word; the first word used should introduce the function being described.

Here is a list of action words that may be referred to when writing job descriptions.

accepts	constructs	files
acts	consults	fills–in
administers	coordinates	fines
advises	corrects	follows–up
allocates	correlates	formulates
analyzes	counsels	furnishes
anticipates	creates	generates
approves	decides	guides
arranges	delegates	identifies
ascertains	deletes	implements
assigns	designs	informs
assists	determines	initiates
audits	develops	inspects
authorizes	devises	instructs
balances	directs	interprets
batches	disseminates	interviews
calculates	documents	investigates
circulates	drafts	issues
classifies	edits	itemizes
codes	ensures	lists
collates	establishes	locates
collects	evaluates	maintains
compiles	examines	manages
conducts	facilitates	measures
consolidates	figures	modifies

monitors	provides	selects
negotiates	pursues	signs
notifies	rates	specifies
observes	receives	studies
obtains	recommends	submits
operates	records	summarizes
organizes	refers	supervises
originates	renders	tabulates
outlines	reports	trains
oversees	represents	transcribes
participates	requests	transposes
performs	researches	troubleshoots
places	routes	types
plans	reviews	utilizes
prepares	revises	verifies
processes	schedules	writes
proposes	screens	

Considering certain questions before actually writing the job description can be helpful.

1. Does the job-holder supervise the work of others? If so, give job titles and a brief description of the responsibilities of those supervised.
2. What duties does the job-holder perform regularly, periodically, and infrequently? List these in order of importance.
3. What degree of supervision is exercised over the job-holder?
4. To what extent are instructions necessary in assigning work to the job-holder?
5. How much decision-making authority or judgment is allowed to the job-holder in the performance of the required duties?
6. What are the working conditions?
7. What skills are required for the successful performance of the job?
8. What authority does the job-holder have in such matters as training other people or directing the work force?

9. At what stage of its completion is the work of the job-holder reviewed by the supervisor?
10. What machines or equipment is the job-holder responsible for operating? Describe the equipment's complexity.
11. What would be the cost to management of serious mistakes or errors that the job-holder might make in the regular performance of the required duties?
12. What employees within the organization and customers or clients outside the organization will the job-holder interact with on a regular basis?

The exact contents of a job description will be dictated by the specific environment and needs of an organization. What follows provides the basic categories of job information required for most positions.

1. Date
2. Job analyst (person who wrote the job description)
3. Job title
4. Division and department
5. Reporting relationship
6. Location of the job
7. Exemption status
8. Salary grade and range
9. Work schedule
10. Job summary
11. Duties and responsibilities, including extent of authority and degree of independent judgment required
12. Job requirements, including education, prior work experience, and specialized skill and knowledge
13. Physical environment and working conditions
14. Equipment and machinery to be used
15. Other relevant factors, such as degree of contact with the public or customers and access to confidential information

A job description form containing these categories appears in Appendix A.

Once a job description is written, review it on a semiannual or annual basis to make certain the nature of the job has not changed substantially.

SUMMARY

In this chapter the steps that should be taken before recruiting job applicants have been examined. These ten steps are:

1. Reviewing the specific job duties and responsibilities
2. Assessing the role of prior work experience and relevant educational credentials
3. Considering intangible requirements
4. Understanding reporting relationships and decision-making roles
5. Becoming familiar with various facets of the work environment, including working conditions, location of the job, travel, and schedule
6. Knowing the exemption status
7. Assessing the salary range
8. Knowing the union status
9. Being aware of growth opportunities
10. Considering any other special requirements

It was further explained that the most comprehensive and expeditious way of accomplishing these steps is via a job description. Having completed the job-familiarization stage, the interviewer is now ready to explore and compare various recruitment sources.

2

Recruitment Sources

Now that you are thoroughly familiar with the details of the available job, it is time to begin screening qualified applicants. Where are these applicants to be found? Numerous sources may be utilized. Some will be more appropriate for nonexempt jobs; some will produce a greater number of applicants than others; some will be very costly; others will take a long time to yield results. All of them have advantages and disadvantages that must be weighed each time there is an opening.

JOB POSTING

Almost without exception, the first recruitment source that should be explored is your own organization. Promoting or transferring employees from within offers several advantages.

1. It will usually create an opening at a lower, easier-to-fill level.
2. The company saves considerable time and money by transferring someone who is already familiar with the organizational structure and methodology.
3. Employee morale is boosted.
4. Hidden talent may be uncovered.

The process by which internal recruitment is accomplished is called *job posting*. With this system, every time a position becomes available it is offered to present employees before recruiting via outside sources. A simplified job description citing the department, location, exemption status, salary grade and range, work schedule, requirements, primary duties and responsibilities, and working conditions is literally posted in one or more centrally located places. Also included is a closing date by which time all applications must be submitted. The standard period of time for this is generally from one to two weeks. Some organizations require that interested employees receive permission from their existing supervisors before applying; others require notification; still others respect the confidentiality of the process until a decision has been reached. A sample job posting notice form appears in Appendix B, and a sample job posting application form is shown in Appendix C.

All applicants are considered in the same manner as any outside candidate would be. If an appropriate person is found, arrangements for a starting date in the new position are made between the existing department head, personnel, and the new department head. Anywhere from two to four weeks is generally allowed for finding a replacement to fill the position being vacated.

Some organizations have a policy of posting all openings; others post only nonexempt positions. Some steer clear of job posting altogether. Reasons for this include:

1. Supervisors and managers sometimes want to promote someone they have groomed for a position. Therefore, they do not want to even consider other candidates.
2. Some members of management get upset with employees who apply for jobs outside of their department and tend to take any such move personally.
3. Losing an employee to job posting may mean having to wait for a replacement who may not be as good.
4. Some companies believe that it is better to bring in "new blood" rather than to recycle existing employees.

The success of a job posting system depends largely on how well it is designed and monitored. For example, an organization may choose to stipulate that employees must be with a company for at least one year and in their current position for at least six months before they may utilize the job posting system. The number of jobs that an individual may apply for within one year is also limited, generally to three. In addition, employees must have received a rating of satisfactory or better on their most recent performance appraisal in order to use the job posting system. These guidelines help prevent the problem of the "revolving door" employee who may opt to apply for virtually every job posted. It also treats the process in a serious manner and lends it credibility, thus increasing its effectiveness.

WORD OF MOUTH

One of the least expensive and most expeditious recruitment sources is word of mouth. As soon as it is known that an opening is to occur the word spreads. The department head tells other department heads; employees talk with one another; word is then carried outside the organization to family, friends, and acquaintances. As an added incentive to help fill the job quickly, some companies offer a bonus to an employee whose recommendation results in a hiring. These bonuses have been known to range from twenty-five dollars to several hundred dollars. Generally, it is required that the new employee remain with the company for at least one year and receive a minimum of a satisfactory rating before the referring employee can collect a large bonus.

On the surface, word of mouth appears to be an ideal recruitment source. It is certainly a highly effective tool, but caution must be exercised in its use. It has been shown that "like tends to refer like." For example, white males tend to refer other white males. The result of this could be the perpetuation of systemic discrimination whereby women and minorities are not afforded an equal opportunity to apply for certain jobs. (See Chapter 4 for more on the law and the employment process.) While there may be not be outright intent to discriminate, the effects of this recruitment process may nevertheless be discriminatory. Hence, word of mouth should be used only in conjunction with other recruitment sources.

ADVERTISING

One popular and often effective means for soliciting applications is advertising in both newspapers and professional publications. Careful planning in terms of content, timing, and location can generate a large response, usually resulting in a hiring.

Consider those you want to reach when designing the contents of an ad. If you are looking for individuals with very specialized skills, the ad should clearly stipulate those skills. If on the other hand you are scouting for talent, the wording of your ad should be less specific. The same holds true for the extent to which you spell out the job's duties and responsibilities. Some employers want applicants to know virtually everything about a job before they apply for it. Others prefer to learn about the candidates and establish interest before describing the details of the job. When advertising, make certain that enough information is provided for applicants to determine whether or not it is worth their while to apply. Also be sure to include how you want to be contacted: resume, telephone call, or walk-in.

A sampling of ads illustrating the range of information offered appears in Appendix D.

Regardless of how explicit you plan to be, it is always best to be direct and straightforward in your wording. Avoid cute or unprofessional phrases. Keep in mind that the way your ad looks and reads is a reflection of your organization. Hence, consider the image you wish to project. You may choose to hire an advertising agency to write the ads, but this is usually not necessary. You know the job better than anyone outside of the organization and therefore, can better describe it. However, assistance from an agency may be desirable in determining such factors as the categories under which an ad should appear, spacing, and the boldness and size of letters.

Agencies may also be able to provide advice as to the best day of the week to run an ad for a specific job category. For example, Wednesday has traditionally been the best weekday on which to run an ad for secretaries in *The New York Times*. The issue of when to run an ad can make a big difference in the number of responses received. Not only can specific days of the week make a difference, but the time of year can also influence responsiveness. Ads run just before Christmas and New Year's Day, for instance, generally do not do well, although during times of high unemployment this is not necessarily true.

Where you choose to advertise will also have an effect on responsiveness. It is a good idea to begin by scouting all the newspapers in your area. Note the propensity for certain jobs to appear in certain publications. Also consider papers that have a very broad appeal, such as *The Wall Street Journal*. This becomes especially important if you are seeking to locate candidates for a hard-to-fill opening. Also consider publications that are read mainly by women or minorities, such as *Black Careers, Equal Opportunity,* or *Nuestro.* Ads placed in these publications can help your company meet its affirmative action goals.

You may choose to advertise in a business magazine if you are not in a hurry to fill a position and can wait for the issue carrying your ad to be published. Most professional journals have a classified section that reaches a wide audience of specialists in a given field and is generally not too costly.

This raises the issue of money. Wordy display ads with large type, logos, and borders can cost a small fortune. Unfortunately, if you are seeking candidates for a highly competitive field, you may need to compete visually with other ads— content alone does not always bring the desired response. However, if you are going to spend a great deal of money, make certain that the ad says exactly what you want it to say. In order to outshine competitors, brag about your outstanding benefits package, starting salary, and any perks you may offer.

Some organizations like to run blind ads. These are ads that do not reveal the company's identity, instead giving a box number to which a resume may be forwarded. This is usually done to avoid having to respond to a flood of phone calls. On the other hand, with hard-to-fill positions where the number of responses will probably be limited, you will want interested individuals to get in touch with you as soon as possible. Blind ads sometimes discourage people from applying altogether. Without knowing who is running an ad, there is always the danger of someone applying to his or her own company for a new job.

As a final comment with regard to advertising, make certain that the language used does not violate equal employment opportunity laws and regulations. This would include stating a preference for either sex, indicating an age preference via terminology—such as "young man" or "mature woman"—or using certain other discriminatory terms—such as "attractive," "pretty," or "handsome." See Chapter 4 for additional information regarding this subject.

EMPLOYMENT AGENCIES AND SEARCH FIRMS

Two additional popular recruitment sources are employment agencies and search firms. Generally speaking, search firms handle only professional openings, while employment agencies recruit for all other types of jobs.

There are two primary reasons why agencies and search firms are frequently used. First, they have access to a large labor pool and can readily scout the market for qualified candidates. Second, they can often help fill a position more quickly than a company could on its own.

The most overwhelming reason for not retaining the services of an agency or search firm is the cost. While each agency's fee structure will differ, they usually work on a contingency basis; that is, they do not collect their fee until a referred applicant is hired. The cost then ranges from 1 percent per each $1,000 of salary all the way up to a straight 25 percent of the annual salary. Executive search firms can charge from 25 to 30 percent of the new employee's salary for the first year. There may be additional charges for related out-of-pocket expenses.

Before agreeing to register an opening with either an employment agency or a search firm, consider the following guidelines.

1. Be certain that the agency will evaluate applicants and refer only those who meet the standards stipulated. Too often agencies will merely forward resumes to a client, expecting the company's interviewer to do the screening.

2. Be firm about the job's requirements and refuse to consider anyone who does not meet them.

3. Ask for a written agreement regarding the fee arrangement, including how much, when it is to be paid, and any other conditions. For instance, some search firms will refund a percentage of the fee paid if employees placed as a result of their efforts are terminated within the first three to six months of work.

4. Be selective in determining which agencies and search firms will receive your business. Meet with and interview representatives in advance to make certain that they clearly understand your objectives. Establish their degree of knowledge in the area for which they will be recruiting, and make certain that you feel comfortable working with them. Ask for information regarding their methodology, experience, and track record. Do not hesitate to ask for references and consider their reputation in the field. Also be sure that the person with whom you meet is the person who will actually be handling your company's account.

5. Formally notify all agencies and search firms with whom you will be working that you are an equal opportunity employer. Also share information regarding your organization's affirmative action plan. Make it very clear that you expect them to comply fully with all equal employment opportunity and affirmative action laws and regulations and that you will terminate your relationship if they should violate these laws at any time.

Once you have decided to work with a particular employment agency or search firm, allow agency representatives to learn as much as possible about both your organization and the specific job opening. The more information the agency has, the better able it will be to meet your needs effectively and expeditiously.

PERSONNEL FILES

Sometimes the expense of an agency or ad can be avoided simply by referring to the company's personnel files. It is quite possible that someone applied for a similar position not too long ago. If the person was not hired, this does not mean that he or she was a poor candidate. It may have been that there were several qualified applicants at the time among whom only one could be chosen. Or perhaps there were no suitable openings when this individual filed his or her application. It is also possible that the applicant's salary requirements exceeded the amount then being offered.

When scanning personnel files for existing applications, carefully compare background and skills with the requirements of the available position. Also review the notes of the previous interviewer and, if possible, talk to him or her in person. Hopefully, the previous interviewer will recall the individual well enough to provide you with additional information.

WALK-INS, CALL-INS, AND WRITE-INS

Three other closely related, valuable recruitment sources that do not cost anything are walk-ins, call-ins, and write-ins. Walk-ins and call-ins usually consist of nonexempt applicants; write-ins are usually professionals. These unsolicited applications can often result in the hiring of outstanding employees. Too often, however, walk-ins, call-ins, and write-ins are not treated seriously. Walk-ins are automatically told by the receptionist that there are no openings at the present time. If they are permitted to complete an application, these forms are quickly filed away without an interviewer ever seeing them. Call-ins are generally told to apply in person. When they do, they are told that there are no openings. Likewise, unsolicited resumes are given a cursory glance at best, and then filed. Sometimes letters of acknowledgment are sent, but more often than not there is no communication whatsoever.

A simply monitored system for handling these types of applicants can yield excellent results. Make certain that the receptionist in the human resource department has an up-to-date list of job openings, accompanied by a simplified job description for each one. Every time a walk-in applies for a job, this list

sidered wasted. Job fairs usually have social functions in the evenings; this is a wonderful opportunity to meet and exchange information with recruiters from other organizations. This type of networking among recruiters often leads to a sharing of resumes and information for hard-to-fill positions later on.

OPEN HOUSE

Another type of recruitment effort occurring outside of the company is the open house. Organizations place ads in newspapers throughout various geographic locations. The ads announce a recruitment drive in these areas on specific dates. Unless the companies are very well known, a somewhat lengthy description appears of the company's product and its reputation in its field. Statements regarding the excellent starting salaries and benefit packages are also included. All available jobs are listed as well.

On the advertised date of the open house, company recruiters gather to greet and interview anyone expressing an interest in working for them. Either decisions are made during this recruitment drive or arrangements are made to have the applicants return to the company at a later date for additional interviews.

An open house is usually a risky proposition in terms of cost and time. It is difficult to predict with any certainty whether there will be a large turn-out, resulting in the filling of several openings, or whether very few qualified people will show up. Prescreening applicants by telephone or asking them to submit resumes in advance are two ways to safeguard against this occurrence.

GOVERNMENT AGENCIES

Another recruitment source is the state or federal employment agency. These agencies are cost-free; they screen and refer many applicants, usually for entry-level or nonspecialized positions. Because they keep such careful equal employment opportunity records, government agencies can be counted on to help your organization meet its affirmative action goals.

An additional advantage is that candidates referred by government agencies are all currently unemployed, which means that anyone you select can usually begin work right away. If the person were currently working, anywhere from one week's to two weeks' notice to his or her current employer would be in order. When you have deadlines to meet and work to get out, those two weeks can seem like an eternity.

While government agencies can be very helpful, they are frequently known to refer unqualified job applicants in spite of the requirements stipulated. In addition, they often challenge the reasons given for rejecting a candidate. Therefore, it is important that recruiters learn appropriate rejection language. This is covered in Chapter 6.

DIRECT MAIL RECRUITMENT

A recruitment source that is less frequently used but that can be very effective is the direct mail campaign, whereby specific individuals are contacted by a company with an opening, hoping for a job match.

The first step in this type of recruitment is determining whom to contact. You will need several different mailing lists to begin with. These lists and list information may be obtained through professional associations, business directories, trade groups, and magazine subscription lists. *Direct Mail List Rates and Data*, published by Standard Rate and Data Service, Inc., 5201 Old Orchard Road, Skokie, Illinois 60077, can offer additional assistance. You may also opt to hire the services of direct mail specialists or consultants to help you plan and implement your mail campaign.

If you are embarking on an extensive mailing effort, it is advisable to have a mailing house help you fold, stuff, seal, and mail everything. If, however, your mailing list is rather small, you can do everything yourself. Obtain a copy of the *Mailer's Guide* from your local post office for guidance.

Direct mail campaigns often fail because recipients do not even open the envelope. Sometimes this problem can be circumvented by putting some sort of attention-getter on the envelope. Teasers, such as "we want to give you $40,000!" are not advisable, as they are unprofessional. Instead, consider printing "personal" or "confidential" on the outside. Not only is it more likely that the addressee will open the envelope, but others, such as clerks or secretaries, are less likely to do so. The letter should contain a clear, brief, easy-to-read message. The first sentence should inform the reader of your purpose and interest. Include information about the requirements of the job, its duties and responsibilities, and its benefits. Try to anticipate any basic questions an applicant might ask and provide answers for these. Enclose a response card or ask to be contacted by telephone. If possible, also provide a flier or brochure about your company.

One final suggestion is to ask for a referral; in the event that your initial prospect is not interested in the position he or she may know of someone who is.

RADIO AND TELEVISION

There are two tremendous advantages to using radio or television advertising to fill an opening. First, you will appeal to a very large audience in a very short period of time. Second, you can reach and tempt prospects who are not actually looking for a job. These advantages may be offset, however, by the cost involved. Even one radio or television spot can be very expensive. In order to be effective, your message should be repeated frequently, so your expenses will add up quickly.

To get your money's worth, make certain that your message is convincing. The speaker's voice in a radio or television ad should be sincere and pleasing to the ear. The appearance of your television spokesperson should be professional. No matter how short your ad may be, make it a point to repeat the name of your firm and how you may be reached. In the interest of time and money, offer a telephone number, as opposed to an address. A telephone number will also be easier to remember in the event that the viewer or listener does not have a pad and pen handy.

COMPUTERIZED SYSTEMS

One final source of potential employees is computer-based recruitment. This type of system matches jobs with viable candidates. Computers can be very helpful in finding qualified applicants, often in much less time than any of the other means described. Some of these systems put candidates directly in contact with prospective employers; others act as a liaison, contacting companies as applicant representatives. To utilize this method of recruitment employers will need both hardware and appropriate software.

In considering a computerized recruitment system certain factors should be reviewed. These include:

1. How up-to-date the information on candidates is.
2. How many candidates are generally available for each job field (data bases of about 500 applicants per job field are considered to be good).
3. How efficient the system is in terms of distinguishing the most qualified candidates.
4. How cost-effective the system is in relation to other recruitment sources.
5. How much time will be saved by using a computerized system. In this regard, look for services that offer on-line access 24 hours a day.
6. How difficult the system is to operate.
7. Confidentiality of information for both the employer and the applicant.
8. How adaptable the system is to existing equipment.

Some organizations choose to develop a computerized recruitment system in-house. They usually purchase a prede-

Table 2-1. Advantages and disadvantages of the various recruitment sources.

Recruitment Source	Advantages	Disadvantages	Level of Positions
Job posting	Creates openings at lower, easier-to-fill levels Saves time and money Boosts employee morale Reveals hidden talent	Managers feel they can no longer select persons of their choice Managers resent employees who want to post for jobs outside of their department Time may be lost waiting for replacement	Nonexempt and exempt
Word of mouth	Inexpensive Expeditious Related bonus boosts employee morale	May result in charges of systemic discrimination if not used in conjunction with other recruitment sources	Nonexempt and exempt
Advertising	Reaches a wide audience Can solicit responses via blind ads Magazine ads zero in on specific occupation categories	Can be very costly Can delay filling of a position	Nonexempt and exempt
Employment agencies and search firms	Access to large labor pools Can help fill position quickly	Can be very costly Can refer unqualified applicants	Employment agencies nonexempt; search firms exempt

Table 2-1. (continued)

Recruitment Source	Advantages	Disadvantages	Level of Positions
Personnel files	No cost Good public relations	If on a manual system, can be time consuming Poor notes taken by the previous interviewer may cloud applicant desirability	Nonexempt and exempt
Walk-ins, call-ins, and write-ins	No cost Good public relations	Poorly monitored system can result in lost applicants Interviewing walk-ins and talking with call-ins can disrupt interviewers' work schedule	Walk-ins and call-ins nonexempt; write-ins exempt
Campus recruiting	Opportunity to groom and develop future management of a company Opportunity to select top graduates	Costly Fatigue Must evaluate potential, as opposed to concrete work experience	Exempt
Job fairs	May fill many openings in a short period of time	Costly Usually means working on a weekend	Exempt

Method	Advantages	Disadvantages	Classification
Open house	Opportunity to network with other recruiters Good public relations May fill several openings at one time	Fatigue Costly Time-consuming	Exempt
Government agencies	Cost-free Can result in referral of many applicants Can help with affirmative action goals Can help fill positions quickly	May send unqualified applicants May challenge reasons for rejection	Nonexempt
Direct mail	Personalized form of recruitment Selective	Time-consuming Costly	Exempt
Radio and television	Reaches a wide audience Can help fill positions quickly	Costly	Nonexempt
Computerized systems	Can help fill positions quickly Extensive data base	Requires specific hardware and software Can be costly	Exempt

veloped package from an outside vendor and then proceed to implement and monitor it internally. However, most companies utilize the services of an outside firm. Payment for services is on either a monthly or an annual basis for limited or unlimited use of the system. Since this is a relatively new source of recruitment the actual cost varies greatly. If you believe that your company might benefit from this service, take time to examine exactly what you will be getting for your money.

SUMMARY

This chapter explored thirteen different recruitment sources. Table 2-1 summarizes the advantages and disadvantages of these sources.

With all the different recruitment sources available, you should never find yourself in the position of saying, "I can't find anyone to fill this job." If this occurs, it is probably because the job expectations are unrealistic. Nor should you ever feel pressured into taking the first person who applies for an opening because you feel desperate. This often backfires when the person hired quits or is fired for poor performance in a short period of time. You are then in a position of having to recruit all over again.

By exploring the various sources described in this chapter you can afford to be selective. The investment in time and money will pay off when you find the best person for the job.

3

Preparing for the Interview

Once the recruitment process is underway and qualified candidates are scheduled, you can concentrate on preparing for the actual face-to-face interview. Careful attention to this important phase of the employment process will result in a smoother, more effective meeting with applicants and ensure selection of the best possible employee.

REVIEW THE APPLICATION AND RESUME

Begin the preparation stage with a review of the completed application form and/or resume. This step should never be omitted, even if you are interviewing walk-ins or are running behind schedule. Take the time necessary to review all applicants' backgrounds and qualifications before seeing them. Experienced interviewers find that they can review the application as they walk from their office to the reception area to greet the candidate.

There are two reasons for doing this. First, you will become familiar with the person's credentials, background, and qualifications as they relate to the requirements and responsibilities of the position; second, you will be identifying questions to ask during the interview.

Many clients ask me to describe the contents of an ideal application form. My response is that although all application forms should contain certain specific questions, each organization should have one that reflects its own environment and individual needs. For example, the application form for a highly technical company will differ from one used by a nonprofit organization. Some companies have more than one form: one that is used for professional or exempt positions and another that is used for nonexempt positions.

Appendix E illustrates a job application form containing questions that might be used in most organizations. Review its contents with your own organization in mind, modifying it as required.

When designing an application form it is important to remember that all categories must be relevant and job-related. This is critical from the standpoint of compliance with equal employment opportunity laws. Interviewers should note that familiarity with federal laws is not sufficient, since many state laws are more stringent. Therefore, compliance with federal regulations could still mean violation of state regulations. Where there is a difference, the stricter law prevails. Oversight or ignorance of the law does not provide immunity.

Even the simplest application form has numerous categories that should be reviewed before a face-to-face interview. The same holds true for resumes. As you review these categories keep in mind that a completed application form or resume that deviates from the acceptable format does not automatically mean that the candidate should not be considered for the position. The way in which people present themselves on paper is only one of the factors that you should consider when making your hiring decision.

Be aware that resumes differ somewhat from applications, in that people start with a blank piece of paper, as opposed to a form with specific questions to be answered. Consequently, on their resumes people offer whatever data they choose. Generally speaking, the same basic information should appear on a resume as appears on an application form. This includes work history (i.e., employer, location, duration, duties, and special accomplishments), educational degrees, and scholastic achievements. Career objectives may be cited and a list of the applicant's publications may also be included. Usually, professional candidates who submit resumes are also asked to complete an application form, although not until after a hiring decision has been reached.

Following are ten key areas to focus on when reviewing

an application or resume. A completed application form illustrating these areas appears in Appendix F.

1. Scan the overall appearance of the application or resume. Check to see that it is neat and easy to read. Applications can be typed or handwritten, and should be legible. Resumes should always be typed and then printed up as opposed to photocopied. The contents of applications and resumes should be grammatically correct and the language easy to understand. Resumes are generally one to two pages in length and sometimes have writing samples attached. They should be professional in appearance and not made to capture your intention with garish colors, clever phrases, or scented paper. Although they are not essential, cover letters usually accompany resumes and show added interest on the part of the applicant.

2. Look for any blanks or omissions. This is easy with an application form; with a resume, check to see that basic information (work and educational history) has not been excluded. Make a note of any missing information so that you can ask the applicant about it. Some employment application forms are poorly designed, causing candidates to inadvertently overlook certain questions. Or it may be that an applicant purposely omitted certain information. If this is the case it is up to you to find out why and to determine the importance of the missing data.

3. Review the applicant's work history and make a note of any time gaps between jobs. A gap of more than one month should be accounted for. If an applicant states that he or she took some time off between jobs to travel throughout Europe make a note of it. Be careful that you do not pass judgment, deciding that this was a frivolous and irresponsible pursuit. Fill in the gaps and worry about drawing conclusions after the interview process is completed.

4. Consider any overlaps in time. For example, the dates on an application may show that the candidate was attending school and working at the same time. Of course, this is possible, but not if the school happens to be in California and the job was in New York. Even if the locations are consistent, you need to verify the accuracy of the dates.

5. Make a note of any other inconsistencies. To illustrate, let's say there is an applicant with an extensive educational back-

ground who has been employed in a series of nonexempt jobs. This may be because he or she has degrees in a highly specialized field and cannot find suitable work. It is up to you to find out if this is the case.

6. Next consider the frequency of job changes. People voluntarily leave jobs for many reasons including an inaccurate description of the work at the time of hire; an improper job match; personality conflicts on the job; inadequate salary increases; limited growth opportunities; and unkept promises. Some employees who know that they are doing poorly will voluntarily terminate their employment just prior to a scheduled performance evaluation. Then there are instances when an employee is let go. This may occur when a firm shuts down for economic reasons; when major organizational changes cause the deletion of several positions; or when a temporary assignment has been completed and there is no additional work to be done. Of course, employees are also terminated for reasons such as poor performance or excessive absenteeism.

When reviewing a candidate's employment record it is important that you do not draw premature, negative conclusions regarding the frequency of job changes. To determine what constitutes a frequent change is highly subjective. Too often interviewers set arbitrary guidelines, sometimes patterned after their own work history. You may decide that changing jobs more often than once every two years is too frequent and that this translates into unreliability. However, at this stage of the interview process you simply do not have enough information to make such a decision. After all, you have not even met the applicant yet. Make a note that you want to discuss his or her pattern of job changes and move on to the next category: salary history.

7. In our society it is assumed that everyone wants (and needs) to make more money. Indeed, it is one of the most commonly cited reasons for changing jobs. However, you will undoubtedly come across applicants who are willing to take a job at a lower salary than they were previously or are presently earning. The reasons for this vary. Sometimes an individual wants to move from one area of specialization to another and recognizes that his or her lack of expertise in the new field will mean less money—something they are willing to contend with

in order to make the change. Sometimes people want to work for a particular company and are willing to earn less in order to do so. Then again, some people simply do not care about money all that much. They only want to have enough to meet their basic expenses and are not concerned with luxuries. For them, job satisfaction is of paramount importance. Then there are those individuals who have been unemployed for a long period of time and cannot find work at their old rate of pay. They may be willing to work for less until they can get back on their feet. Once again, you must be careful not to draw conclusions. At this point all you should do is explore this area so that you can put together the pieces after the interview.

8. Carefully review the candidate's reasons for leaving previous jobs. Look for a pattern. For example, if the reason given for leaving several jobs in a row is "no room for growth" it may be that this person's job expectations are unrealistic. This explanation for leaving could also be a cover-up for other, less-acceptable, reasons. Of course, it may also be perfectly legitimate. Whatever the explanation may be, this is a key area to explore in the face-to-face interview.

9. Job titles may also require explanation. Some titles are not functional or descriptive in nature and, therefore, do not reveal an incumbent's general realm of responsibility. Examples of such titles include *administrative assistant* and *vice president*. Sometimes titles sound very grand, but upon probing, you may discover that they carry few responsibilities. If the person's duties are not clearly described on the application or resume make a note to ask for elaboration.

10. Review the application or resume for any "red-flag" areas. This is any information that does not seem to make sense or that leaves you with an uneasy feeling. A classic example is the response to the category *reason for leaving last job*. The popular answer "personal" should alert you to a possible problem. Many interviewers assume that they have no right to pursue this further—that to do so would be an invasion of the person's privacy. This is not true. You have an obligation to ask the applicant to be more specific. Of course, if people begin to volunteer truly personal information about their home life and personal relationships then you must interrupt and ask them to focus on job-related incidents that may have contributed to their

decision to leave. Also note that "personal" is frequently a cover-up for "fired." Many applicants count on interviewers not going any further upon seeing the explanation "personal" and, therefore, use this term instead of revealing that they were asked to leave their last job.

If the applicant becomes uncomfortable as you try to discover what "personal" really means it is suggested that you stop and come back to this area later in the interview, perhaps after a better rapport has been established. You must make it clear to an applicant that the information is vital for continued consideration. Often this message will be sufficient to encourage even the most reluctant applicant to provide a full explanation. You may also have to pose very specific questions, instead of simply asking the applicant to elaborate. For instance, you might ask if the departure had anything to do with the immediate supervisor, the working conditions, fellow employees, or benefits. Another way to encourage the applicant to reveal this information is to tell the person that a reference check will be made and that the former employer will be asked why he or she left.

Skilled interviewers know how to ask questions, are sensitive to body language (their own and that of the applicant), and are aware of the impact of tone of voice and the importance of rapport. They will eventually obtain the information they are seeking.

Applications and resumes are full of information for you to pursue during the course of the interview. Because they are the foundation of the selection process it is critical that you take time before meeting with a candidate to clearly identify those areas that need to be investigated further.

ALLOW SUFFICIENT TIME FOR THE INTERVIEW

The next step in the interview preparation stage has to do with the amount of time allotted for each interview. In considering this, think about the entire interview process and not just the portion devoted to the face-to-face meeting. Time is needed *before* the interview to review the application and/or resume, as already described. Time is also needed *during* the interview for you to ask questions of the applicant, provide information about the job and the company, and allow the applicant to ask questions. Finally, time is needed *after* the interview to write up your notes, reflect on what took place, set-up additional appointments, and check references. Additional time may be needed before or after the interview for testing.

Considering all that must be done, just how much time should be set aside for each interview? There is no single correct answer. Much depends on the nature of the job; that is, whether it is nonexempt or exempt. Generally speaking, more time is needed for interviewing professionals: usually a total of 90 to 120 minutes. This amount of time should be sufficient for you to ascertain the necessary information about a candidate's qualifications and to get a good idea of job suitability and applicant interest. If the actual face-to-face interview runs much beyond 90 minutes it becomes tiresome for both the applicant and the interviewer.

In the case of interviews for nonexempt positions approximately 45 to 60 minutes should be allotted, with 30 to 45 minutes for the face-to-face meeting. More concrete areas are usually probed at this level (i.e., specific job duties, attendance records, and the like). These take less time to explore than the numerous intangible areas examined at the exempt level, such as management style, level of creativity, and initiative.

The time frames discussed here should only be used as guidelines. Be flexible in the actual amount of time allotted, but also be aware of these general parameters because they can help you to ascertain sufficient information and to avoid discussing irrelevant factors. For example, if you find that your interviews are over within 15 minutes this is generally because you are not phrasing your questions properly; that is, you are asking yes/no questions as opposed to open-ended questions (See Chapter 5). It may also be that you are not adequately probing suspicious areas, as described earlier in the chapter, or perhaps you simply do not know what questions to ask. If, on the other hand, your interviews last much beyond 45 minutes for a nonexempt position or 90 minutes for an exempt position, it is likely that the applicant has taken control of the interview. When this occurs, interviewers often find themselves describing their own career with the company at some length. They may also find themselves discussing the contents of books on their shelves or explaining pictures and photos on their desks. It is not unusual for inexperienced applicants to try to steer interviewers away from questions regarding their job suitability. By diverting the interviewer's attention and talking a blue streak about irrelevant matters, applicants hope to cloud the real issue of whether or not they are qualified for the job. Of course, some people simply like to talk a lot and do not intend to be devious. Regardless of the motive, however, interviewers are cautioned against allowing applicants to take control of the interview. This is less likely to happen if you are aware of the appropriate time frame for an interview.

PLAN AN APPROPRIATE ENVIRONMENT

Once you have blocked the necessary amount of time for your interview, plan the environment in which it will be conducted. Here are some guidelines to consider.

1. *Ensure privacy.* This is very important if applicants are expected to talk freely. They must be assured that what they are saying cannot be overheard by others. This is particularly important when they are discussing sensitive matters, such as why they are being asked to leave their present jobs.

2. *Ensure a minimum number of distractions.* These would include your phone ringing without someone answering it for you, people walking into your office, and your own menta distraction as you think about all the work you have to do.

3. *Make certain that the applicant is comfortable.* This does not require fancy furniture, oriental rugs, or a fireplace. Your behavior and general approach to the interview will largely determine the comfort level of the applicant. If you can offer the

applicant a choice of seats, fine. If, however, space is limited and there is only one other chair, that is all right also, as long as you put the applicant at ease. Take his or her coat, make certain that the chair is not stacked with books and magazines, and offer a beverage if possible. Do whatever you can to create a comfortable environment. If the applicant feels comfortable, you will be assured of a more productive interview.

4. *Consider the seating arrangements.* There is no one proper relationship between your seat and the applicant's seat. Some interviewers feel that desks create a barrier between themselves and the applicant. If this is how you feel, then the desk does indeed become a barrier. However, if you are comfortable seated behind your desk, then by all means sit there. The applicant will undoubtedly feel comfortable on the other side of the desk in this instance.

BE CLEAR ABOUT YOUR OBJECTIVES

As part of the interview preparation stage it is important that you remind yourself of exactly why you are conducting these interviews. What are your objectives? Always start by examining the large, overall picture and consider your organization's goals. Ask yourself: What kind of place do I work in? What is the atmosphere like? What is the image that my company wants to project? What kind of employee does this organization want to hire?

Next consider the divisional and departmental goals, both short- and long-term. Consider what type of employee is going to be of help in achieving these goals. Also carefully consider the personalities of the manager and the other employees in the department where the opening exists. While skill and experience are the main factors used to evaluate an applicant, an individual's style of working can clash with that of others in the department. For example, someone who works best independently and without direction would not fare well in a unit with a hands-on supervisor who not only wanted to know what his or her employees were doing at all times but also wanted to be actively involved in the actual work.

PLAN YOUR BASIC QUESTIONS

Next consider the basic questions to be asked. In addition to reviewing the completed application and/or resume for areas to be pursued and developed, you should plan a handful of general questions. These will serve as the foundation for your interview. The job description is an excellent source for this type of question. By reviewing the job description you can easily identify what skills are required. Then proceed to formulate the questions you will need to ask in order to determine whether or not applicants possess these skills and are capable of performing the required duties and responsibilities. Hypothetical situations can also be developed from this, which can then be presented to candidates to enable them to demonstrate their skills and potential.

Be careful not to list too many questions or become very specific during this stage of preparation. If you have an extensive list of detailed questions, the tendency will be to read from that list during the interview. This will result in a stiff, formalized session, which could conceivably make the applicant feel ill-at-ease. In addition, with a lengthy list of questions interviewers feel compelled to cover the entire list, and often end up being redundant. Again, this can result in the applicant feeling uncomfortable and wondering whether or not you are really listening to his or her responses.

Limit yourself to about a half-dozen general questions. Once you get into the interview the other questions that need to be asked will follow as offshoots of the applicant's answers. In fact, if your first question is a good, open-ended question, the applicant's response should provide you with numerous additional questions to ask. An example of an effective first questions might be, "Would you please describe your activities during a typical day on the job?" As you listen to the applicant's response, note any areas that he or she mentions that you want to pursue further during the course of the interview.

CONSIDER HOW THE APPLICANT MAY BE FEELING

Another aspect of the preparation phase to consider is how applicants may be feeling just prior to being interviewed. It is not uncommon for candidates to experience emotions such as anxiety, fear, nervousness, and intimidation as they sit waiting to be evaluated. It is very difficult to assess job suitability when an applicant is experiencing such negative feelings. Therefore, it behooves you to put forth a little bit of extra effort in establishing a rapport at the outset of the interview. This will help the applicant feel more comfortable and better able to communicate with you. Be particularly sensitive when there is a great deal of competition for a single opening, as it is especially hard for an individual to feel confident under these circumstances.

Furthermore, if you are relaxed and express interest in the candidate and do not permit distractions or interruptions during the course of the interview, then the odds are that the applicant will relax as well. Remember, the best interviewer is the one who empathizes with how the applicant is likely to be feeling.

PERCEPTION

One last area to consider before you actually conduct an interview is the role of perception. This is a critical phase in the objective evaluation of job candidates. Before meeting an applicant interviewers should briefly review the five ways in which we formulate our perceptions and ideas about people.

1. *First impressions.* This is the most prevalent and often the most damaging way of formulating our ideas about people, since we often form first impressions without even realizing it. Interviewers who are unaware of the importance of perception frequently boast, "The minute he walked in the door, I could tell he was right/wrong for the job."

This is a mistake. You cannot determine job suitability by

sizing someone up in a split second based on his or her appearance. Of course, appearance, which consists of many components including clothing, colors, and grooming, does play a role in the selection process. After all, employees represent an organization and therefore, the image that they project is a direct reflection on that company. The problem is that interviewers have a tendency to form preconceived notions of how employees in certain job classifications should look. An accountant, for example, conjures up a different image than a mechanic. If a person applying for a mechanic's opening came to an interview dressed in a suit and tie, you would be surprised but probably not turned off. However, if an accountant appeared in your office wearing overalls, it is far more likely that you would form a negative first impression. This is because we tend to have very specific impressions of how an employee in a particular job category should look. We also fail to consider that the applicant may have a reason for dressing a certain way. It is possible that at the applicant's former place of employment a casual style of dress was acceptable.

First impressions should play a role in your decision-making process, but not at the exclusion of all the other factors to be examined. Do not allow them to act as a substitute for judgment. Try not to form a first impression until after you have conducted the interview. You may find that the applicant's attire or grooming is the only problem. The person's job skills may be superior to those of all other candidates. At this point you can talk to the applicant about the desired image of your organization. Then schedule a brief follow-up interview to see if your message was clearly received.

2. *Information from others.* An applicant who comes highly recommended by someone for whom you have high regard can elicit a positive response from you prior to the actual face-to-face meeting. On the other hand, someone you dislike may make a referral to you, and thereby automatically create a negative bias toward the person being recommended. In both instances you are allowing yourself to be influenced by information from others. Instead of assessing the applicant on his or her own merits, you are assessing the person making the recommendation, thereby transferring your opinion from the referral source to the applicant. Like first impressions, informa-

tion from others does play a role in the decision-making process. Anything that might supplement the data on an application or resume can be helpful, but it is premature to make an evaluation based on this highly subjective aspect of perception at this stage of the employment process.

3. *Single statements.* Suppose an applicant's response to one of your questions rubs you the wrong way. If you are not aware of the impact that a single statement can have, it could bother you to the extent that you eliminate the person from further consideration. This might occur even though the comment does not constitute a valid reason for rejection. You must be particularly careful if this should happen during the initial stage of the interview, when you are trying to put the applicant at ease and establish rapport. This is commonly accomplished through a few minutes of small talk (See Chapter 5). During this portion of the interview you might comment about some political news that caught your eye in the morning newspaper. The applicant might then express his or her views on the subject, which happen to be contrary to yours. If you are not careful, you could allow this difference to influence your objectivity in assessing the applicant's job suitability. You will then have taken a single statement—one that is totally irrelevant to the decision-making process—and allowed it to affect your judgment.

Even those single statements that *are* job-related must be weighed in relation to other qualifying factors. Keep in mind that it should usually be a combination of factors that results in the rejection of a candidate.

4. *Body language.* Nonverbal communication is a vital aspect of the employment process. Often an interviewer can learn as much about an applicant through his or her nonverbal messages as can be learned from verbal ones. This topic will be explored more fully in Chapter 5. However, it is important at this point to recognize body language as one of the components of perception. Nonverbal messages that are misinterpreted by the interviewer can result in poor selection or rejection decisions. This usually occurs when body language is interpreted according to the interviewer's own gestures or expressions. For example, just because you have a tendency to avoid eye contact when you are hiding something does not mean that the applicant

is avoiding your eyes for the same reason. It may very well be a sign that he or she is deep in thought.

Each of us has our own pattern of nonverbal expression, attributable to a combination of cultural and environmental factors. These factors influence such elements of body language as gesture, posture, touching, and the distance we maintain from one another. With regard to the latter, referred to as *proxemics*, our culture recognizes a distance of from two to five feet as being an appropriate distance between interviewer and applicant. A candidate from a culture that regards this as too much distance might immediately pull his or her chair up much closer to the interviewer. This might be interpreted as a violation of space or as an act of aggression or intimacy, leaving the interviewer with feelings of discomfort, hostility, or intimidation.

Another aspect of nonverbal communication—*chronemics*—has to do with the amount of time that passes between verbal exchanges. In our culture we expect people to respond to our questions immediately. In other cultures people deliberately wait before answering. An applicant who does this might be perceived by his or her interviewer as being bored, inattentive, confused, or nervous.

Be careful not to draw conclusions too early in the interview process, based on an applicant's nonverbal messages. Allow time for the individual's patterns to emerge, and then relate these patterns to the other factors involved in making a selection.

5. *Ethnocentrism.* This is the final aspect of how our perception of others is formed. Ethnocentrism means that we use our values, standards, and beliefs to judge or evaluate others. Overall, this is a perfectly natural result of the cultural conditioning process that we are all exposed to. In our early years we are taught by well-intentioned parents, teachers, and religious leaders to think and act according to certain standards and values. At the age of five or six few of us question the validity of these standards. Unfortunately, many people grow up believing that these are the only acceptable standards. This results in stereotypical thinking. Consequently, we assign specific attributes and roles to others, based on surface characteristics, such as sex, age, or ethnic origin.

Other factors come into play. For example, the interviewer

sees from a resume that the applicant graduated from the same college that he or she attended. On the basis of the interviewer's fond memories and high regard for the school, certain positive qualities about this candidate may erroneously be assumed. Or perhaps the resume shows that the applicant attended Harvard. The interviewer's general assumptions about Harvard graduates could lead him or her to hastily conclude that the person would fit in.

Negative reactions may also occur. For instance, a candidate may presently be working for an organization from which your brother was recently fired. This negative association could bias your assessment of the applicant's job suitability. When perceptions are based on ethnocentric thinking objectivity falls by the wayside. The chances for open, effective, communication are blocked whenever an applicant's response or nonverbal messages deviate from the interviewer's preconceived notions. Keep in mind that ethnocentrism does not pertain to work-related standards established by the company; rather, it comes into play in the intangible areas of an individual's style and approach. It is in direct opposition to objectivity, which is an interviewer's number one obligation.

The five aspects of perception—first impressions, information from others, single statements, body language, and ethnocentrism—together become a valuable tool in the preparation stage of interviewing. Briefly reviewing them just prior to meeting with an applicant can help you avoid hasty hiring or rejection decisions based on nonfactual, subjective factors.

SUMMARY

This chapter has outlined the steps required to prepare for the face-to-face interview. In summary, they are as follows:

1. Review the completed application form and/or resume.
   a. Scan the overall appearance.
   b. Look for blanks or omissions.

    c. Look for gaps in time.
    d. Consider overlaps in time.
    e. Note any inconsistencies.
    f. Consider the frequency of job changes.
    g. Consider salary requirements.
    h. Review reasons for leaving previous employers.
    i. Review job titles.
    j. Explore "red flag" areas.

2. Block sufficient time before, during, and after the interview.
3. Establish an appropriate environment for the interview.
4. Be clear about your objectives.
5. Plan your basic questions.
6. Consider how the applicant may be feeling.
7. Consider the role of perception:

    a. First impressions.
    b. Information from others.
    c. Single statements.
    d. Body language.
    e. Ethnocentrism.

Taking the necessary time to go through this process will yield excellent results as you approach each interview prepared to select the best possible candidate.

4

Interviewing and the Law

There is one final area of preparation required before proceeding with the actual interview: familiarization with equal employment opportunity (EEO) laws and regulations. This area is not restricted to human resource professionals. Anyone having anything to do with recruitment, interviewing, or selection of personnel is expected to have a basic knowledge of EEO and its impact on the employment process. Ignorance of the law or unintentional violations do not provide immunity.

It is impossible to incorporate everything about EEO into this book. Included will be highlights of relevant legislation and categories of discrimination. The impact of EEO on the employment process will be described, and specific examples of acceptable and unacceptable interview inquiries will be provided. A brief discussion of preemployment testing will also be offered. Readers are urged to keep abreast of news regarding this ever-changing field. One source for this is the *Personnel Manager's Legal Reporter*, a newsletter issued on a monthly basis by the Bureau of Law and Business, Inc. The bureau is located at 64 Wall Street, Madison, Connecticut 06443. A yearly subscription costs $72.00. Your daily newspaper will also contain information regarding recent EEO lawsuit settlements and changes in legislation. When in doubt as to the suitability of an interview question or any activity related to the hiring process check with the EEO officer in your organization before proceeding. The information contained in this chapter is current as of late 1985.

EEO LEGISLATION AND AFFIRMATIVE ACTION: CATEGORIES OF DISCRIMINATION

Generally speaking, EEO legislation exists to ensure all individuals the right to compete for all work opportunities without bias because of their race, color, religion, sex, national origin, age, or handicap. Such laws have been in existence in this country for nearly 120 years, dating back to Section 1981 of the Civil Rights Act of 1866. This early piece of legislation was originally intended to support charges of race discrimination in employment situations, and was expanded in 1982 to include national origin discrimination as well. It applies to all employers regardless of the number of employees.

There have been numerous additional laws passed since the Civil Rights Act of 1866. Perhaps the best known is the Civil Rights Act of 1964. Title VII of this act prohibits discrimination on the basis of race, color, religion, sex, or national origin. It is important to note that this pertains to all facets of the employment process and not just to recruitment and hiring. The criteria for coverage by Title VII includes any company doing business in the United States that has 15 or more employees. Violations are monitored by the Equal Employment Opportunity Commission.

Following the Civil Rights Act of 1964 acts of discrimination continued. The excuse most commonly offered by employers was that while they certainly did not intend to discriminate, they simply could not find women and minorities for their job openings. The result of this frequently-repeated statement was a revamping of recruitment sources. Up to this point the most popular, cost-effective means of recruitment was word of mouth. The inherent problem with this method was that whenever there was an opening at a supervisory or managerial level—the level at which women and minorities were so few in number—the existing managers, predominately white males, spread the word among close friends and colleagues: other white males. Not surprisingly, the candidates referred were more white males. Therefore, the word-of-mouth system was inherently discriminatory when it was the only method of recruitment used. Recruitment sources were subsequently expanded to include many of those identified in Chapter 2.

Even after recruitment sources were expanded discrimination continued. However, employers no longer claimed that they could not find women and minorities to hire. The problem, they now claimed, was that they could not find *qualified* women and minorities. A close examination of most educational and experiential requirements revealed unrealistic standards that were not necessary for the successful performance of the job. It was also true that because of the limited educational and employment opportunities afforded women and minorities, few individuals who fell into these two categories possessed the stipulated qualifications.

The result of this close examination of position qualifications was a revamping of job requirements. An employer could no longer arbitrarily decide that a degree was necessary for a given position. It now had to be shown that a person without a degree could not do the job. Individuals with an equivalent combination of education and experience had to be considered. Likewise, an arbitrarily set number of years of prior experience was eliminated and replaced with more realistic requirements. Phrases such as "extensive experience required" became increasingly popular.

In addition, a series of Executive Orders was issued by the federal government. The best known, E.O. 11246, contained an EEO clause that asked companies doing business with the federal government to make a series of promises. Three of these promises are detailed here.

1. The first promise concerns nondiscrimination. When you do business with the federal government you are making a contract with them; should you discriminate in your employment practices you would effectively be violating your contract. The ramifications of this could be severe, including contract cancellation and debarment, meaning that the government would no longer do business with your company.

2. The second promise you make when doing business with the federal government is to obey the rules and regulations of the Department of Labor. This promise extends to allowing periodic checking of your premises by labor representatives to assure compliance.

3. The third promise is called *affirmative action*. This means that you are committed to hiring, training, and promoting a certain percentage of qualified women and minorities. The actual percentage is based on the number of women and minorities in your particular geographic area. These are your affirmative action goals. Separate affirmative action plans are required for each establishment: a business location having some component that exercises personnel authority and responsibilities. No separate plan is required if the location has less than 50 employees or if two locations are in the same Standard Metropolitan Statistical Area.

Affirmative action is a way of ensuring minimal compliance with EEO. Franklin A. Thomas, the first black president of the Ford Foundation, said in a speech he gave at the 1982 Granada Lecture Series in England, "Affirmative Action is really a way to introduce us to each other. . . . One day our descendents will think it incredible that we once made so much out of such small things as the amount of melanin in our skin or the shape of our eyes or the single element of gender in the complex human being."

The most recent set of requirements for a written affirmative action plan, set by the Office of Federal Contract Compliance Programs, pertains to employers with at least 100 employees and $100,000 in federal government contracts. However, it is strongly recommended that employers have a written plan even if they do not fit this description. Having a written plan and a proven commitment to achieving the goals set is often viewed as an important effort in precluding discriminatory practices. Many cases involving employment discrimination do not develop beyond the initial stages because of the existence of such a demonstrated effort. The plan must be *practiced* however, and not just written.

Thus far, only two major pieces of EEO legislation have been mentioned, along with affirmative action. There are a number of other acts that anyone involved in the employment process must be familiar with. Failure to comply with these laws could result in costly litigation. Readers are urged to consult with in-house or outside counsel in the event that they are charged with discrimination.

As the following fair employment laws and categories of discrimination are outlined, bear in mind that they are federal regulations; as mentioned in the previous chapter, state laws may differ and should also be considered.

The Equal Pay Act of 1963

The Equal Pay Act of 1963 requires equal pay for men and women performing substantially equal work. The work must be of comparable skill, effort, and responsibility, performed under similar working conditions. This law protects women only. Criteria for coverage is at least two employees.

Unequal pay for equal work is permitted in certain instances, for example, when wage differences are based on superior educational credentials or extensive prior experience. It should be noted that coverage applies to all aspects of the employment process including starting salaries, annual increases, and promotions.

An important issue related to equal pay is *comparable worth*. Currently, about a half dozen states have implemented programs for comparable worth pay whereby employers are required to compare completely different job categories. Those held predominately by women (e.g., nursing and secretarial), must be compared with those occupied predominately by men, (e.g., truck driving and warehouse work). Point systems determine the level of skill involved in the job, as well as the economic value of each position. If the female-dominated jobs are deemed comparable, pay adjustments are made to reduce the difference in wages.

The important distinction between comparable worth and equal pay is that in order to claim violation of the Equal Pay Act identical job classifications must be compared. Therefore, if a female accountant believes that she is not receiving an equal rate of pay to that of her male counterpart—a male accountant who is performing substantially equal work—she could conceivably have sufficient cause to claim violation of the Equal Pay Act. On the other hand, comparable worth allows comparison between different job categories. For example, if a clerk-typist believes that her work is of comparable worth to her employer as that of a male custodian working for the same employer, she might sue on the basis of sex discrimination. Since there is presently no federal law regarding comparable worth, she would sue for violation of Title VII of the Civil Rights Act of 1964.

In August of 1985, the Equal Employment Opportunity Commission stated that it would not consider "pure" comparable worth cases. This was a reversal of the commission's previously stated intention to implement a comparable pay doctrine requiring employers to reevaluate the worth of their positions and eliminate salary discrepancies between traditionally male and female jobs. The following month the nation's first statewide ruling requiring comparable pay for jobs of comparable worth was overturned by a federal appeals court. This reversed a decision worth potentially $1 billion to approximately 15,500 women in the state of Washington.

Although the controversy over comparable worth continues, companies are urged to voluntarily assess their hiring practices and work toward minimizing specifically female or male categories.

The Age Discrimination in Employment Act

The federal Age Discrimination in Employment Act (ADEA) of 1967, which was amended in 1978, protects workers from ages 40 to 70. The criteria for coverage is at least 20 employees. It is important to note that many state regulations covering age discrimination have no age limit whatsoever. If two people are both in a protected age group, an employer can not favor the younger of the two. Therefore, a 41 year-old employee may not be favored over a 60 year-old employee.

Want ads should be carefully reviewed to spot language that may be designed to attract either younger or older workers. Phrases such as *college student*, or *supplement your pension* clearly show a preference for individuals in certain age categories and should be avoided.

The Rehabilitation Act of 1973

This law protects qualified handicapped individuals against discrimination in employment. The term *qualified* means capable of performing the essential functions of the job. The term *handicapped* refers to individuals inflicted with physical or mental disabilities or impairments, and includes those who are classified as alcoholics or drug addicts. Obesity is also considered an impairment. An employer's obligation with regard to a qualified handicapped applicant or employee is to make every effort to accommodate the person's handicap, as long as such accommodation does not create an undue hardship. Undue hardships are determined by considering such factors as the size of the organization, the type of work involved, and the nature and cost of such accommodation. For example, job restructuring might be required if the handicapped person can perform the essential functions of the job, but requires assistance with one remaining aspect of the work, such as heavy lifting. Other aspects of job restructuring may be developing new career paths for handicapped individuals, relocation, modification of procedures, providing readers or interpreters, or modification of equipment. Any adjustment that does not create an undue hardship may be required.

Alterations to facilities (e.g., the installation of ramps, special parking, and new means of access to buildings) may also be required. Compliance with the *American National Standard Specifications for Making Buildings and Facilities Accessible to, and Usable by, the Physically Handicapped*, published by the American National Standards Institute, Incorporated, is required.

With regard to positions requiring tests, if the handicapped applicant cannot take a required test, he or she must be allowed to demonstrate the ability to perform the essential functions of the job through alternative means.

Also relevant to the subject of the handicapped is the issue of preemployment physicals. Generally speaking, if your organization has been conducting preemployment physicals as a matter of past practice, then there is no problem with continuing to do so. However, if this has not been the case and you want to start requiring physicals, you must prove necessity. In addition, physicals must be required for everyone; you cannot require physicals only for the handicapped. Furthermore, the physical cannot be the first step in the application process. It may either be the last factor evaluated or it may be required after a conditional job offer is made.

Determining an individual's physical fitness for work must be done by a qualified physician. Any negative findings should be phrased in specific, objective, job-related terms. The results of the examination must be shared with the applicant. If the applicant can do the job that he or she is interviewing for, but you fear that employment will aggravate an existing condition, you are on weak ground if you deny that person employment. You are on stronger ground if the condition is degenerative in nature. If the applicant can do the present job, but can probably not do the next job in the promotional chain, you may be able to deny employment if you can document that promotion is the normal pattern in a particular job family.

The Pregnancy Discrimination Act of 1978

The Pregnancy Discrimination Act of 1978 states that pregnancy is a temporary disability and that pregnant women may not be singled out for special treatment. If you are going to have special rules for pregnancy, be prepared to prove that they are dictated by business necessity or related to issues of safety or health. Women must be permitted to work as long as they are able to perform the essential functions of their jobs. Therefore, you may not arbitrarily set dates for beginning maternity leave. Your policy must allow each woman to tailor her schedule to her own physical condition. You may not refuse to hire an applicant who is pregnant unless she cannot perform the essential functions of the job.

Religious Discrimination

According to the Civil Rights Act of 1964, Sec. 701 (j), "The term religion includes all aspects of religious observance and practice, as well as belief. . . ." What this essentially means is that an individual need not be affiliated with a large, popular, well-known, religious sect in order to maintain that some aspect of your employment practice interferes with his or her religious beliefs.

The most recent revisions to the federal guidelines on religious discrimination make it illegal to discriminate against anyone with regard to their religious convictions in any aspect of the employment process. This means that all preemployment inquiries concerning availability on, say, Saturdays or Sundays, must be job-related, dictated by business necessity, and worded in such a way that availability is stressed, as opposed to specific questions about religion. Therefore, if a given position requires working on Sunday, you might phrase your inquiry in this way: "This job requires working on Sunday. Is there any reason you would not be able to meet this job requirement?" Or, "Will you be able to meet this job requirement?" If the applicant responds by saying, "No, I cannot work on Sunday, because of my religion," then a number of things should follow. First, it is recommended that you confirm his or her response by repeating your original question: "Are you then saying that you cannot meet one of the requirements of this job, which is to work on Sundays?" When the applicant repeats his or her response, document this as part of your interviewing notes by writing in very simple and clear language, "Applicant is unable to meet the job requirement of working on Sundays." Do not make any reference to the reason given, which is religion.

Your next step is to try and make a reasonable effort to accommodate this person's religious practices as long as they do not create an undue hardship for you, the employer. Reasonable efforts might include finding voluntary substitutes for the period of time when this individual would be unavailable; flexible scheduling of hours so that his or her religion could be accommodated; consideration of another position with comparable salary, responsibilities, working conditions, location and growth opportunities; or perhaps hiring a temporary employee to cover the person's duties during the time when he or she would be unable to work. As with accommodating the handicapped, just what would constitute an undue hardship depends on a number of factors, including prohibitive cost. Generally speaking, the larger the company, the more you are expected to be able to spend for accommodation. Undue hardship must be provable. The size of your organization is again taken into consideration—the larger the company, the harder it is to prove hardship in terms of time, resources, and money.

Remember that you are not automatically obliged to hire someone whose religious convictions interfere with or do not fit in with job specifications. Employers *do* have the right to require quiet and unobtrusive observance. However, you must try to accommodate a person's religion as best you can.

National Origin Discrimination

The EEOC's "Guidelines on Discrimination Because of National Origin" preclude denial of equal employment opportunity because of an individual's ancestry, place of origin, or because an individual has the physical, cultural, or linguistic characteristics of a national origin group. There are two main areas of concern which pertain to hiring.

1. *Citizen requirements.* Citizen requirements may not be valid if they have the purpose or effect of discrimination on the basis of national origin.

2. *Selection criteria.* Selection criteria that appear to be neutral on first glance may have an adverse impact on certain national groups. This would be true, for example, of height and weight requirements.

Sexual Harassment

The 1980 guidelines issued by the EEOC regarding sexual harassment define it as unwelcome sexual advances, requests for sexual favors, or other unwanted verbal or physical conduct of a sexual nature. In order to be considered a violation of Title VII of the Civil Rights Act of 1964, submission to or rejection of such conduct must be made a term or condition of employment.

Reverse Discrimination

This is the final major category of discrimination that will be mentioned. Reverse discrimination occurs when whites—usually white males—believe that they have been denied equal employment opportunity because of favoritism shown to minorities and/or women. This occurs most frequently when affirmative action programs have the effect of limiting employment and promotional and training opportunities for nonminorities.

THE IMPACT OF EEO
AND AFFIRMATIVE ACTION
ON THE EMPLOYMENT PROCESS

It is important to understand just how all of these EEO and affirmative action laws affect recruitment, hiring, and selection. As the employer you have the right to select whomever you believe is best qualified to perform the duties and responsibilities of a given job. You are not required to select the *most* qualified person; rather, you are required to select someone who meets the minimum requirements of the job. Your responsibility does not end there, however; other factors must be considered. First, check yourself to make certain that you are not denying anyone equal employment opportunity, either inadvertently or because of personal bias. Second, check your employment practices for possible systemic discrimination. Third, make certain that your requirements are job-related and not arbitrarily set. Finally, be aware of your organization's affirmative action goals and take them into consideration when weighing the qualifications of women and minorities versus white males. Full compliance with your affirmative action goals is your objective, and you should make every effort to achieve this end whenever you have an opening to fill.

If after considering all of these factors and assessing both the tangible and intangible qualifications of all your candidates, you determine that the most suitable person for the job is someone who happens to be a white male, you are free to make that person a job offer. However, if the credentials of two candidates—one a white male and the other a minority member or a woman—are essentially the same, and your affirmative action goals are not yet adequately met, you are urged to hire the minority member or the woman.

BONA FIDE OCCUPATIONAL QUALIFICATIONS

Occasionally the requirements of a position seem to be discriminatory in nature. For instance, jobs that stipulate male or female only, clearly appear to be discriminatory. However, upon closer investigation it is sometimes evident that the EEO concept of bona fide occupational qualification (BFOQ) prevails. By definition, a BFOQ is a criteria that appears to be discriminatory but can be justified by business necessity. For example, an employer may have an opening for a model to demonstrate a designer's new line of dresses. In this instance being female would be a BFOQ. An example of an unacceptable BFOQ would be a position requiring heavy lifting where only male applicants were considered. The requirement of lifting may be tested; all applicants—male and female—could be asked to lift the amount of weight that would normally be required on the job. Those that were unable to perform this task would not be considered. This would include all men who did not meet the requirement, as well as all women. Likewise, women who could lift the weight would have to be given an equal opportunity for the job.

Bona fide occupational qualifications may apply to religion, sex, and national origin, but never to race. Furthermore, general company preference does not constitute a legitimate BFOQ. The most valid BFOQ or business-necessity defense is safety.

When in doubt, the following business-necessity action guidelines should serve to help you.

1. Document the business necessity.
2. Explore alternative practices.
3. Ensure across-the-board administration of the practice.
4. Be sure that the business necessity is not based on stereotypical thinking, arbitrary standards, or tradition.

Remember, there are very few instances in which BFOQ apply. If you believe that you have requirements that qualify, it is recommended that you check with your company's EEO officer before proceeding.

PREEMPLOYMENT INQUIRIES

Most people have a general idea as to what categories to steer clear of during the employment interview. They know that questions relating to race, color, religion, sex, national origin, and age should be avoided. Some questions, however, have traditionally been considered acceptable during an interview, and the reader may not realize that they are discriminatory in nature.

Before proceeding with the identification of these inquiries it is important to note that asking these questions is not, in and of itself, illegal. Rather, once you have ascertained the information, you may be charged with illegal use of it. For example, asking a female applicant if she has children is not an illegal question. However, if you decide not to hire this person because she answers affirmatively and you anticipate excessive absenteeism, then you may be charged with discrimination.

Also bear in mind that just because you do not directly ask an applicant—either via the application form or verbally—for specific information, he or she may offer it. If this occurs, you are equally as liable if a question of illegal use arises. For instance, suppose that you inform an applicant that the position for which she is being considered involves travel. You then ask if she foresees any problem in being able to leave for a business trip with very little advance notice. She responds, "Oh, that will be no problem at all. My mother has been baby-sitting for my three kids ever since my divorce last year." The applicant has just volunteered information regarding two categories that are not job-related: children and marital status. If she is rejected, she might conceivably claim discrimination on the basis of this information, even though you did not solicit it.

Should a candidate provide you with information that you know you should not have, make certain of three things: first, do not, under any circumstances, write the information down; second, do not pursue the subject with the applicant; and third, tell the applicant that the information is not job-related and that you want to return to discussing his or her qualifications in relation to the job opening.

Table 4-1 lists the most common categories and questions to avoid during the employment interview, both verbally and via the application form. Related recommended inquiries and categories of discrimination are also shown. Many of the rec-

(*Text continues on page 72.*)

Table 4-1. Preemployment inquiries.

Category of Inquiry	Inquiries Not Recommended	Recommended Inquiries	Categories of Discrimination
Name	What is your maiden name? Have you ever used any other name? Have you ever changed your name?	Have you ever worked for this company under any other name? Is there any information relative to a change of name that would help us in conducting a reference check?	Women Minorities
Address	Do you rent, or own your own home?	Where do you live? How long have you lived there?	Women Minorities
Age	How old are you? What is your date of birth? Are you between 18–24, 25–34, etc.? Proof of age.	Are you between age ____ and ____? (depending on state law) Are you above the minimum working age and below the mandatory retirement age?	
Physical appearance	How tall are you? How much do you weigh?	No inquiries pertaining to physical appearance, unless they are BFOQs	Women National origin

Citizenship and national origin	Of what country are you a citizen? Where were you born? Where were your parents born? Are you a naturalized or a native-born citizen? What is your nationality?	Are you a U.S. citizen? If you are not a U.S. citizen do you have the legal right to remain/work here? Do you intend to remain in the U.S.?	National origin
Marital status	What is your marital status? Do you wish to be addressed as Mrs., Miss., or Ms.?	No inquiries pertaining to marital status	Women
Children	Do you have any children? How many children to you have? What child-care arrangements have you made?	No inquiries pertaining to children	Women
Police records	Have you ever been arrested?	Have you ever been convicted of a . . . . (crime? felony? crime greater than a misdemeanor?)	Minorities

Table 4-1. (continued)

Category of Inquiry	Inquiries Not Recommended	Recommended Inquiries	Categories of Discrimination
Religion	What is your religious background? Is there anything in your religious beliefs that would prevent you from working on a Saturday or a Sunday?	No inquiries pertaining to religion. If information regarding weekend availability is needed, ask: Is there any reason you would be unable to work on (Saturday/Sunday) as required of this job?	Religion
Disabilities	Do you have any disabilities? Have you ever been treated for any of the following diseases?	Do you have any physical, mental or medical impairments that would interfere with your ability to perform the job for which you are applying? Are there any positions or duties for which you should not be considered because of medical, physical, or mental disabilities?	Handicapped

Subject			
Photographs	Any requirement that a photo be supplied before hiring	Statement that a photo may be required after hire	Women Minorities
Language (if job-related)	What is your native language? How did you learn a foreign language?	What language do you speak, read, or write fluently? What is the degree of fluency?	National origin
Relatives	Who should we notify in the event of an emergency? Any inquiry calling for the names, addresses, ages, number, or other information regarding the applicant's relatives not employed by the company	Do you have any relatives, other than a spouse, already employed by this company?	National origin
Military experience	Have you ever served in the armed forces of any country? What kind of discharge did you receive from the service?	Have you ever served in any of the U.S. military services? Describe your duties while in the U.S. service	Women Minorities National origin

Table 4-1. (continued)

Category of Inquiry	Inquiries Not Recommended	Recommended Inquiries	Categories of Discrimination
Organizations	What clubs or organizations do you belong to?	What professional organizations, trade groups, unions, or other organizations, relative to your ability to perform the job for which you are applying, do you belong to?	Women Minorities National origin
References	A requirement that a reference be supplied by a particular kind of person, for example, a religious leader	Names of individuals willing to provide character or professional references	Women Minorities

Finances	Do you have any overdue bills?	No inquiries regarding an applicant's financial status	Women Minorities
Education	Are you a high school/college graduate?	What is the highest grade that you completed? What academic, vocational, or professional schools have you attended and when?	Women Minorities
Experience	Any inquiry regarding non-job-related work experience	Describe your prior work experience, especially as it relates to the position for which you are applying	Women Minorities

ommended inquiries appear on the application form in Appendix E.

EDUCATION AND EXPERIENCE

At this point it may appear that there is very little that you can ask an applicant. While it is true that there are many categories of information that interviewers must avoid, the categories of education and experience will provide most of the information needed to make an effective hiring decision, without violating any EEO laws. Chapter 5 provides a lengthy list of questions developed from these two areas.

Here are some EEO-related guidelines to keep in mind when setting educational and experiential requirements.

1. Make certain that all educational requirements are job-related. It has been shown that high school diploma requirements have a greater negative impact on minority members than on anyone else. This is because, historically, minority members have not had the same educational opportunities as others. In order to require a high school diploma it must be relevant to the job. Do not rely on subjective judgment. Ask yourself whether there is good objective documentation that supports the claim that a high school diploma is necessary in order for an employee to perform the duties and responsibilities of the job. If there is no such documentation, do not have this be a requirement.

2. With regard to college degrees the same basic guidelines apply. However, since college degrees are usually required for higher-level positions with less tangible requirements, the guidelines also tend to be somewhat less tangible. For example, degree requirements are permitted when the consequences of employing an unqualified person are grave, especially when public health or safety are involved. Also, positions requiring a great deal of personal judgment often have degree requirements, as well as those requiring knowledge of technical or professional subject matter. Furthermore, when it is difficult to make a reliable assessment of an applicant's absolute qualifi-

cations, the degree requirement may provide an adequate substitute mechanism.

3. Although at first glance it appears that it is relatively safe to require a degree, be careful. The burden of proving job-relatedness may easily be yours. The less tangible your reason, the more difficult this will be. It is often wiser to state "degree preferred" or "degree highly desirable." Even better, is to clearly spell out exactly what knowledge and skill level you are seeking. This way, individuals who may have additional years of experience or who may have attended college without receiving a degree, will not be locked out of consideration. You are helping yourself, as well, by not narrowing the field of choice.

4. Also be certain that educational requirements are relevant to the position for which the applicant is applying. In situations where the degree is not necessary for the immediate job, but *will* be required for future jobs to which the employee will be expected to progress, you may have the requirement, if the job is a true stepping-stone. To be on the safe side, it is even better if your organization offers educational assistance, so that the employee may acquire the necessary educational supplements while working for you.

5. Be careful about changing educational requirements. If you have an opening with specific requirements and find someone that you want for the job who does not quite measure up, do not lower the requirements. If you do so, you are leaving yourself wide open to discrimination charges by other applicants. Also, if you have an opening with set educational requirements and an applicant meets them, but you decide in retrospect that the requirements are not stringent enough, you are asking for trouble. If you want to change educational requirements once they are set, you must reevaluate the entire job in relation to the specific duties. Only then can you properly determine whether or not the educational requirements warrant adjustment.

6. As with education, the main criterion for previous work experience requirements should be job-relatedness. The standards should never be arbitrary, artificial or unnecessary.

7. Generally speaking, the more complex the job, the more reasonable it is to have experiential requirements. However, if

you have not required specific experience in the past and the job has not changed substantially in terms of its level of responsibility and specific duties, do not initiate such requirements now. If you do so, it is conceivable that women and minorities will suffer more than white males; in other words, the new requirements may have a greater negative impact on women and minorities. The greater the disparity, the greater the burden will be on you to prove the necessity of the requirements.

8. Also be careful about asking for a specific number of years' experience. It is difficult to prove that four years is not adequate and five years is. How did you determine this? It is not enough to say that the previous incumbent had five years prior experience and did a fine job. Nor is it sufficient to say that a previous incumbent had only four years experience and required a great deal of on-the-job training. It is dangerous to use the performance of specific individuals as the basis for your reasoning. It is also difficult to justify a preference for someone with a little more experience, as opposed to just enough. In such a case, say that five years experience is preferred, not required. Remember, it is not only unwise, from an EEO standpoint, to ask for a specific number of years of experience; you may also be preventing yourself from hiring someone who actually strikes you as the best candidate. If he or she has less experience than required, you cannot safely select them over someone who does meet your stated requirements.

TESTING

Testing is an additional category that must be considered in the light of EEO before proceeding with the actual face-to-face interview. Testing guidelines apply to all selection procedures, including, but not limited to, written tests. Other procedures, including the interview, are considered tests as well.

Tests have been deemed appropriate measures of job performance as long as they do not have an adverse impact on the employment of members of protected groups. The definition of an adverse impact with regard to testing is a selection rate for any group that is less than 80 percent of the rate for the group with the highest rate of selection (white males). To make certain that your selection procedures do not have an adverse impact certain tests must be validated. This involves the assembling and assessment of statistical data. For example, a written test may be given to all applicants for a specific job over a period of several years. Although the test results are *not* considered when selecting employees for the position, they are reviewed and measured against successful job performance by the incumbents. Thus, validation studies demonstrate that the test is a valid predictor of job success. Over a period of time, sufficient data will have been gathered so that the test may be considered validated, and from that point on it may be used as a criterion for selection. You may also use validation studies conducted by others, provided that the jobs they are used for match those for which samples were gathered.

Not all selection procedures must be validated. For example, the face-to-face interview and certain tests of specific skills or abilities, such as typing and shorthand, are perfectly acceptable. However, selection procedures not requiring validation must still follow certain guidelines, with uniformity and job-relatedness being the key ingredients. These guidelines are as follows.

1. The same general areas of inquiry should be explored with all candidates applying for the same job.
2. There must be a single standard for rating scores in tests of skills or abilities such as typing and shorthand.
3. Members of certain groups should never be tested exclusively (e.g., testing only women for typing skills).
4. Tests should be objectively administered by skilled personnel.
5. The same test must always be given in the same environment under the same conditions.
6. If for any reason a test is given twice to one applicant, all applicants must be given the opportunity to take it twice.
7. Instructions for tests must contain clear and simple lan-

guage that members of all ethnic groups are likely to understand.
8. Each applicant must have the same amount of time in which to complete a test.

Adhering to these guidelines for administering a test could help you avoid costly EEO-related problems.

Summary

This chapter has provided an overview of important EEO and affirmative action legislation.

1. Categories of discrimination were described.
2. The impact of EEO on the employment process was examined.
3. Bona fide occupational qualifications were discussed.
4. Specific questions to avoid were listed.
5. Aspects of educational and experiential requirements were explored.
6. Preemployment testing guidelines were outlined.

Interviewers are reminded to keep up to date on EEO and affirmative action revisions. The importance of familiarity with this aspect of interviewing cannot be stressed enough.

5

Conducting the Interview

Having followed the steps outlined in the preceding chapters you are now prepared to conduct the face-to-face interview. It is a good idea to briefly review the major components of these steps just prior to each meeting. This may be accomplished by asking yourself a series of questions.

1. Am I thoroughly familiar with the specific duties and responsibilities that the employee will be required to perform?
2. Do I know what educational and experiential requirements are needed to successfully perform the essential functions of the job?
3. Am I familiar with the type of individual who will be most compatible with the job?
4. Am I familiar with the reporting relationships that relate to the available position?
5. Can I accurately describe the work environment to the applicant in terms of working conditions, location, required travel, and schedule?
6. Do I know the exemption status of this job?
7. Do I know the salary range for this position?
8. Is this a union position?
9. Can I describe the position's growth opportunities to the applicant?
10. Have I thoroughly reviewed the completed application form and/or resume, identifying areas requiring discussion?
11. Have I allowed sufficient time for the interview?
12. Is the environment in which the interview will be conducted comfortable and private?

13. Do I clearly understand the departmental and organizational goals as they relate to this position?
14. Am I aware of the role that perception plays in the interview process, in terms of first impressions, information from others, single statements, body language, and ethnocentrism?
15. Have I planned the basic questions to be asked of each applicant?
16. Have I considered how the applicant may be feeling and what I can do to make him or her feel more comfortable?
17. Am I thoroughly familiar with EEO and affirmative action and their impact on the employment process?
18. Are the educational and experiential requirements of this job in compliance with EEO regulations?
19. Are there any BFOQs for this position?
20. Do I know which questions might be considered discriminatory in nature?
21. If there are any tests required as part of the selection process for this job, have they been validated?

ESTABLISHING THE FORMAT

Now you are ready to consider the format or structure of the interview. It is important to develop a system with which you feel comfortable. It is equally important that the format be practical and that it incorporate all the necessary, concrete components of an interview. These components are:

1. Asking the applicant questions about his or her education and prior work history as it relates to the requirements of the job
2. Providing information about the job opening
3. Selling the company, in terms of its salary and benefits package, growth opportunities, and the like
4. Allowing the applicant to ask questions
5. Telling the applicant what will happen following the interview

Many interviewers believe that it is best to begin the interview by providing information about the job and the company before asking the applicant any questions. They do this for three primary reasons.

1. By providing this information at the outset, they are less likely to forget something.
2. If they wait to cover these areas until the end of the interview, they may run out of time.
3. The interviewer doing most of the talking at the beginning of the interview will make the applicant feel more at ease.

This procedure has one major drawback: providing too much information about the job before the applicant describes his or her capabilities often gives away the job. In many cases interviewers describe the kind of person they are looking for to such an extent that applicants can simply repeat this information later on in the interview when describing their skills. If the interviewer is unaware of what is happening, he or she may erroneously assume that the ideal candidate has just been found.

Some other approaches might be considered instead. One suggestion is to begin by offering some general information about the organization. This might include a brief description of its overall function and any historical information considered interesting. (Note that some interviewers do not like to do this; they prefer to test the applicant's knowledge of the company later on in the interview.) You might also begin by very briefly describing the job opening. This will ensure that the person is applying for the same position that you are prepared to discuss. Or you can start right in with your first question. However, be aware that this can be unnerving if the applicant has not had a chance to get settled.

Some interviewers like a format that begins with a definitive statement as to what will take place. It might go something like this:

Good morning, Mr. Turner. My name is Daniel King. I am going to be interviewing you for the position of Marketing Representative with our company. I will begin by giving you an overview of our organization and then ask you some questions about your background and qualifications. I will then describe the responsibilities of the available position. At that point, I will answer any remaining questions you may have about the job or our company. Before we conclude, I will let you know when you may expect to hear from us.

This is a very formal approach. However, if it is accompanied by the appropriate body language and tone of voice, applicants can be made to feel comfortable. Certainly, with this approach there will be no doubt as to the content of the interview.

Other interviewers have a more relaxed style, and therefore, their format is far less structured. They might begin by saying: "Hi Bob. I'm Dan King. I see you're applying for a Marketing Rep opening. Why don't I talk a little bit about our company and then you can tell me some things about yourself. If you think of any questions as we're talking, just jump right in and ask me."

Still others are extremely flexible and capable of conducting both formal and informal interviews. These interviewers like to quickly assess an applicant's general composure and comfort level while they are waiting to be seen, and adjust their approach accordingly. Applicants who appear to be nervous will be met with a casual, relaxed approach. Candidates who seem rather formal will benefit from a more structured format.

It is important that the system you decide on reflects your own personality and style. If you are more comfortable outlining the format of the interview at the outset, that is fine. If you prefer to begin with a brief overview of the company and the job, and then proceed to ask and answer any questions, filling in as you go along, that will work as well. As long as you feel at ease, the applicant is likely to respond well to whatever format you select.

ESTABLISHING RAPPORT

Regardless of the format you use, take a few moments at the beginning of the interview to establish a rapport with the applicant. This is generally accomplished with ice-breakers: comments and questions that have no real bearing on the job. Their sole purpose is to put the applicant at ease before beginning the actual interview. Here are some popular ice-breakers.

Did you have any trouble getting here?
Were you able to find parking nearby?
How was the traffic getting here?
Were the directions my secretary gave you helpful?
Isn't it a beautiful day?
This is some weather we're having!
Do you think it will ever stop raining?
It certainly is hot today!

Obviously, these are not particularly creative comments or questions; they are not intended to be. In fact, the more neutral they are, the better. At this stage you do not want to discuss any topic that might be considered controversial. This way you will avoid the possibility of forming opinions based on a single, non-job-related statement or being ethnocentric in your interpretation of the applicant's response. Also try to avoid forming first impressions to the extent that they will bias your objectivity. As discussed in Chapter 3, these areas of perception can cloud your ability to judge job-suitability. By adhering to subjects such as the weather and commuting, you should accomplish your goal of relaxing the applicant and establishing rapport without drawing premature conclusions.

Just how much time you should spend on ice-breakers depends on how comfortable the applicant appears to be. In most instances, 15 to 30 seconds is sufficient. Sometimes a little longer will be needed. Under no circumstances should this stage of the interview continue for more than a few minutes. Applicants who are still uneasy after this amount of time will probably not respond to additional small talk. The best thing to do in this instance is to ask your first question.

THE FIRST QUESTION

Getting started with the core of the interview is often difficult. Some interviewers get caught up in small talk and do not seem to be able to move on. Others want to get started but do not know how to make the transition from the ice-breakers to the first important question. Still others simply do not know what to ask first.

For those who get too involved with ice-breakers, it is suggested that you consciously limit your time to two minutes. Be certain to select topics that cannot be developed into lengthy discussions. You may also want to limit yourself to two questions. Self-discipline is the key to succeeding at this.

For those who need help in making the transition from small talk to the first question, consider integrating the topic of your ice-breaker into a transitional statement. For example:

1. I'm glad you didn't have any trouble getting here. I'm anxious to begin talking with you about your interest in our opening for a Marketing Representative.
2. I'm sorry you had trouble finding parking. I know that those meters where you finally found a space allow only one hour. Why don't we get started, so that you can be sure to get back to your car before the meter expires?
3. With the weather so beautiful, I'm sure that you're anxious to get back outside, so why don't we get started?
4. Why don't we get started with the interview; it should help take your mind off the fact that you got soaked coming over here.

These statements create a bridge between one stage of the interview and another, thereby eliminating the awkward silence or stammering that can easily occur.

For interviewers who simply do not know where to begin, consider the question suggested in Chapter 3: "Would you please describe your activities during a typical day on the job?" This question accomplishes a great deal.

1. It helps to relax a still-nervous applicant by allowing him or her to discuss a familiar subject.
2. The open-ended nature of the question encourages the applicant to talk, thereby giving you an opportunity to assess verbal communication skills.

3. It allows you time to begin observing the applicant's pattern of body language.
4. It provides information upon which you can build additional questions.

Of course, this question is not fool-proof. You may find yourself facing an applicant who responds by saying, "Well, that's kind of hard to do. No day is really typical."

When this occurs, be a little more specific in the wording of your question to help the applicant get started. Try adding, "I can appreciate that. Why don't you just pick a day—say yesterday—and describe it for me?"

Once the applicant begins to outline specific tasks, you might interject, "Do you do that every day?" By breaking the question down and encouraging the applicant to talk, you should be able to ascertain the information that you are seeking.

ACTIVE LISTENING

To make sure that you do not miss anything the candidate is saying, it is imperative that you learn and practice active listening skills. Listening to what the candidate says in response to the ice-breaker questions at the beginning of the interview is very different from listening to the answers to questions during the core of the interview. The former is very casual. On the other hand, active listening requires concentration and involves a number of factors. Following here are some guidelines to active listening.

1. *Talk less, listen more.* Most interviewers talk entirely too much. No more than 30 percent of your time should be devoted to talking. This 30 percent should be spent asking questions about the applicant's qualifications, clarifying points, providing information about the job and the organization, and answering job-related questions. The remaining 70 percent of time should be spent actively listening.

2. *Summarize periodically.* Applicants do not always provide complete answers to questions all at one time. Frequently,

you have to bring the pieces together. To make certain that you are doing this accurately, periodically stop and summarize. To illustrate: "Let me make certain that I understand exactly what you have accomplished in this area. You weren't directly responsible for running the department, but your boss was away about 25 percent of the time, and during that time you ran the department. Is this correct?" The applicant may then say: "Well, I didn't exactly run the department; if there were any problems, it was up to me to get in touch with the boss to find out what we should do." This clarification helps you understand the scope and extent of the applicant's responsibility.

3. *Filter out distractions.* This includes people coming into your office, the phone ringing, and having your thoughts focused elsewhere. The last can easily occur when applicants are not interesting to listen to. Maybe the work they do strikes you as being dull, or perhaps they speak in a monotone. When this happens, you may find yourself thinking about your last vacation in the Bahamas and how you wish you were there right now. If you find this is happening, remind yourself that not all positions require effective verbal communication skills. The fact that an applicant is not a skilled speaker may not be a job-related factor. It is unfair to judge someone on the basis of how well they are able to hold your interest. By not actively listening, you are likely to miss important information that could influence your final hiring decision.

4. *Use free information.* Every time an applicant opens his or her mouth, they are giving you free data. If you do not actively listen, you are going to miss valuable information. Free information should be the foundation for many of your interview questions.

5. *Screen out ethnocentric thoughts.* Do not allow personal views or opinions to interfere with active listening.

6. *Use thought speed.* This is a wonderful tool available to everyone. Most people think at a rate of approximately 400 words per minute; we speak at a rate of approximately 125 words per minute. Obviously, this means that we think faster than we can speak, but there is much more to thought speed than this. While the applicant is talking, you can use thought speed to do the following.

a. Prepare your next question
b. Analyze what the applicant is saying
c. Piece together what the applicant is saying now in relation to something said earlier in the interview
d. Glance down at the application and/or resume to verify information
e. Observe body language
f. Consider how this candidate's background relates to the job requirements
g. Take notes

Thought speed can also work against you. This can happen if you: assume that you know how an applicant is going to complete his or her response and tune out before they finish; jump to conclusions too soon; compare a candidate's responses with those of a previous applicant; or get too involved in note-taking.

NOTE-TAKING

It is important for interviewers to understand that active listening does not preclude note-taking. Thought speed allows you to write down key words and ideas during the interview at the same time that you are actively listening to what the applicant is saying. Then, immediately following the interview, you can develop your notes more fully. Doing this right away will insure that you remember important facts. If you have blocked sufficient time for the interview, as discussed in Chapter 3 there should be no problem.

Some interviewers feel that note-taking will offend applicants or make them uneasy. If you believe this to be the case, simply tell the applicant at the beginning of the interview that you will be taking some notes to make certain that you have sufficient information with which to make an effective evaluation. Most applicants not only will not mind, but will prefer it if you take notes. After all, most jobs have many candidates competing for them. With so many people being considered for each position, how can the interviewer differentiate between candidates without notes? In fact, not taking any notes could convey a lack of interest to the applicant and consequently, he or she may not bother putting his or her best foot forward.

Body Language

As discussed in Chapter 3, perception of body language is a vital aspect of the employment process. It can be helpful in clarifying confusing verbal messages and often speaks for itself. It can also easily be misused and erroneously interpreted. Here are some points to remember with regard to body language.

1. Nonverbal communication cannot be universally translated. That is, a gesture that you use to express a certain feeling may mean something entirely different when someone else uses it. For example, in the United States it is commonly assumed that nodding the head indicates an affirmative answer or understanding. However, in the Middle East a single nod means no.

This difference in interpretation does not only occur across different cultures. As a result of our individual socialization processes, each of us develops our own pattern of nonverbal messages. That is, we tend to react to a situation in the same nonverbal way each time that it occurs. For example, the applicant who nervously clasps his or her hands while waiting to be interviewed is likely to do the same thing each time that he or she is nervous. Therefore, although there are no universal interpretations to body language cues, each of us has our own nonverbal pattern that may be consistently translated.

2. Even though there are no universal translations of any one gesture, people tend to interpret certain movements in a given way. The following list illustrates this point.

Nonverbal Message	*Typical Interpretation*
Making direct eye contact	Friendly, sincere, self-confident, assertive

Avoiding eye contact	Cold, evasive, indifferent, insecure, passive, frightened, nervous
Shaking head	Disagreeing, shocked, disbelieving
Yawning	Bored
Patting on the back	Encouraging, congratulatory, consoling
Scratching the head	Bewildered, disbelieving
Smiling	Contented, understanding, encouraging
Biting the lip	Nervous, fearful, anxious
Tapping feet	Nervous
Folding arms	Angry, disapproving, disagreeing, defensive, aggressive
Raising eyebrows	Disbelieving, surprised
Narrowing eyes	Disagreeing, resentful, angry, disapproving
Flaring nostrils	Angry, frustrated
Wringing hands	Nervous, anxious, fearful
Leaning forward	Attentive, interested
Slouching in seat	Bored, relaxed
Sitting on edge of seat	Anxious, nervous, apprehensive
Shifting in seat	Restless, bored, nervous, apprehensive
Hunching over	Insecure, passive
Having erect posture	Self-confident, assertive

Interviewers are cautioned against assigning a specific meaning to a given movement until they can be fairly certain that they are correct. This is another reason why applicants cannot be sized up within the first few minutes of an interview, and why interviews should last for at least 30 minutes.

3. Be aware of sudden changes in body language. For example, if an applicant has been sitting quite comfortably for 20 minutes or so, and then suddenly shifts in his or her seat when you ask why he or she left his or her last job, this is a clue that something is amiss. Even if the applicant offers an acceptable response without hesitation, the sudden change in body language should tell you that something is wrong. Additional probing is necessary. The conflict between the verbal and the nonverbal must not be ignored.

4. Also be careful not to erroneously interpret a person's body language according to his or her reaction to your body language. If you are not aware of your own body language, you may incorrectly assume that an applicant is initiating a nonverbal message, instead of reacting to your own. It is critical to be aware of your own body language in terms of how you react to certain emotions or situations.

Your nonverbal responses can be controlled once you are aware of them. It is important to do this during an interview, since your goal is to evaluate the applicant as objectively as possible. It is difficult enough to make a value judgment; adding elements that may not be valid can only serve to make it harder. For example, suppose that you had a fender-bender on the way into work and consequently, are in a bad mood. If you are not conscious of the body language that you are projecting as a result of this mishap, the applicant may assume that you are reacting negatively to something on his or her resume or to something that he or she has said in response to one of your questions. This is perfectly understandable. After all, how many of us are so secure or self-confident that we would think, "Oh, I know it couldn't possibly have anything to do with me."

5. Also remember that when it comes to perception versus how you really may be feeling, it is perception that counts. To help you understand this point, ask a friend or colleague to observe you during the meeting or throughout a typical work day. Periodically ask for feedback. Ask the person what he or she perceives your mood to be at a given moment based on your body language. Remember, the interpretation may differ

from what you are actually feeling. This simple exercise can help you understand your patterns, and thus help you control your body language during an interview.

6. By being aware of your own body language you can consciously choose to project certain nonverbal messages to applicants. For example, by knowing that nodding one's head is generally interpreted as a sign of understanding, you can use this gesture to encourage an applicant to continue talking. Likewise, if you are aware that leaning forward in one's chair implies interest or attentiveness, you can assume this position when interviewing in order to indicate interest in whatever the applicant may be saying.

ENCOURAGING THE APPLICANT TO TALK

One of the greatest challenges for an interviewer is encouraging an applicant to talk. Of course, some applicants are well-prepared, self-confident, and more than willing to converse with you. Indeed, it is difficult to prevent some of them from talking too much and for too long. With others, however, talking to an interviewer can be intimidating and unnerving; regardless of how much they may want the job, selling themselves may be very difficult for them. Therefore, you must help them. After all, if an applicant does not talk, how can you evaluate job-suitability? Here are five ways in which you can encourage an applicant to speak freely.

1. One technique is repetition. This encourages the applicant to continue talking and also helps to clarify certain points. Repeating the last few words of an applicant's statement and letting your voice trail off as a question mark will encourage the person to elaborate. For example, suppose that the last point an applicant made was: "The most difficult part of being a manager was that I was in charge of 25 people." You could follow-up by saying: "You supervised 25 people . . . ?" The applicant might then reply: "Well, not directly. I was in charge of three supervisors, each of whom monitored the work of about seven workers." To further clarify, you might then say: "So, you

were directly responsible for supervising three people. Is this correct?" The applicant would then state, "Yes, that is correct, although my supervisors always came to me when they were having trouble with their workers."

This dialogue presents a far more accurate picture of the applicant's supervisory responsibilities than the original statements that were made. Using repetition encouraged the applicant to provide valuable additional information.

2. A second technique that may encourage the applicant to talk is summarization. Like repetition, this allows the candidate to clarify the points made thus far in the interview, and to elaborate as is necessary. It further ensures an accurate understanding on your part. Summarization may be used at specific time intervals in the interview, (e.g., every 10 to 15 minutes or after a certain topic has been discussed). For instance, you and the candidate may have just devoted approximately 15 minutes to reviewing his or her prior work experience as it relates to the available position. At that point, you might say: "Let me make certain that I understand what you have said thus far. All of your employment since graduating high school has been as a mechanic. This includes the time that you spent in the Marine Corps. You enjoy this line of work and want to continue doing it. However, you feel that you were underpaid at your last job and that's why you left. Is this correct?"

The applicant can now confirm all or part of what you have just summarized. Be careful not to include more than four or five statements in your summary. This way, if part of it is inaccurate or requires clarification, it will not be difficult to isolate. Also, in order to ensure accuracy, make certain to employ the active listening guidelines outlined earlier in this chapter.

3. Employing certain phrases can also encourage an applicant to continue talking. These phrases include: "I see." "How interesting." "Is that right?" "Really?" and "I didn't know that." It is important to note that none of these phrases express an opinion or show agreement or disagreement; they merely show interest and understanding.

4. In order for these phrases of understanding to be effective they must be accompanied by encouraging body language. Examples of body language that will usually be interpreted as

showing interest are nodding, smiling, direct eye contact, and leaning forward.

Conveying these nonverbal messages consistently throughout the interview will establish your interest in what the applicant is saying, thereby helping the person to provide additional information.

5. One final tool that may be utilized in encouraging applicants to talk is silence. Most people find silence to be awkward and uncomfortable. Consequently, interviewers often feel compelled to talk whenever the applicant stops talking. However, unless you are ready to ask another question, talking when you need additional information from the applicant is not going to help you to make a hiring decision. When the applicant stops talking and you want him or her to continue, try silently counting to five before speaking. This pause often compels a candidate to go on. Of course, you must be careful not to carry silence too far. The interview can easily become a stressful situation if you simply continue to stare at an applicant who has nothing more to say or needs your help. However, if you combine silence with positive body language, the applicant should continue talking within a few seconds. Silence very clearly conveys the message that more information is wanted.

DIFFERENT TYPES OF INTERVIEW QUESTIONS

Although all of the factors discussed thus far are critical for effective interviewing, success often depends on the specific type of question asked. There are six main categories of questions that are commonly used by interviewers. Generally speaking, any thought can be expressed in each of the six ways. The wording you choose for each question will essentially determine how much valid information you receive.

1. *Close-ended questions.* These are questions that may be answered with a single word—generally yes or no. They may also offer multiple choice answers. With regard to the latter, care must be exercised not to offer too many choices; two or three are the most effective number. For example, "Would you

describe yourself as a team-player or an independent worker?" is more effective than, "Which one of the following terms best describes you? (a) Team-player, (b) Lone ranger, (c) Leader of the pack, (d) An idea person, or (e) Follow the leader." In general, however, even limited multiple choice questions should be avoided, since they force applicants to choose, as opposed to allowing them to offer information.

Close-ended questions have limited use. They may sometimes be helpful when an interviewer wants to know certain information at the outset. For instance, an interviewer may be aware that the starting salary for a given opening is very low and that many applicants have expressed a lack of interest in the job upon hearing what the rate of pay is. Therefore, it may make sense to mention this fact at the beginning of the interview: "Are you aware that the salary for this job is $250 per week?" This is a close-ended question, which will elicit a straightforward yes or no response. The answer will determine whether or not it makes sense to continue with the interview.

For the most part, virtually every question that may be asked in a close-ended way can be reworded as a more effective open-ended question. This point will be illustrated shortly.

2. *Probing questions.* These are questions that allow the interviewer to delve deeper for needed information. They are usually short and simply worded. Following are some effective probing questions.

Why?
What caused that to happen?
Under what circumstances did that occur?
Who else was involved in that decision?
What happened next?

Interviewers are cautioned against asking too many probing questions in a row, as they tend to make applicants feel defensive. In addition, accompanying body language should express interest and not seem accusing. Gestures such as narrowing eyes and raising eyebrows should be avoided when asking probing questions.

3. *Hypothetical questions.* These questions can become valuable interviewing tools. Hypothetical situations based on spe-

cific job-related facts are presented to the applicant for solutions. The questions are generally introduced with words and phrases like: "What would you do if . . ."; "How would you handle . . ."; "How would you solve . . ."; "In the event that . . . ."

Although the answers to hypothetical questions can yield information about an applicant's reasoning ability and thought process, care must be taken not to expect "right" answers. Without being familiar with the organization the applicant can only offer responses based on his or her previous experiences.

4. *Loaded questions.* These are questions that force an applicant to choose between two undesirable alternatives. For instance, the question, "Are you the union-organizing type or are you antiunion?" puts the applicant on the spot. Perhaps he or she is neither. However, since the interviewer has only offered these two choices, the candidate may not want to appear contrary and is therefore likely to select the one that most closely reflects his or her views. Loaded questions do not provide any valid information about an applicant and should be avoided.

5. *Leading questions.* Leading questions imply that there is a single correct answer. The interviewer sets up the question so that the applicant provides the desired response. Here are some examples.

You do intend to finish college, don't you?
Don't you agree that most workers need to be watched very closely?
When you were in school, did you waste your time taking art and music classes?

It is obvious from the wording of these questions that the interviewer is seeking a particular reply. When leading questions are asked the interviewer cannot hope to learn anything about the applicant.

6. *Open-ended questions.* These may be described as questions that cannot be answered by a yes or no, and they are clearly the most effective questions that an interviewer can ask. They yield the greatest amount of information and allow the applicant latitude in responding. They also permit the interviewer to assess verbal communication skills and to observe the applicant's pattern of body language. Most importantly, open-ended ques-

tions provide information upon which interviewers can build additional questions.

There are two possible problems with open-ended questions. The first is that the applicant's response may include information that is irrelevant or that violates EEO laws. As soon as this occurs the interviewer must bring the applicant back to the focus of the question. One way to do this is to say: "Excuse me, but we seem to have strayed from the original question of why you left your last job. I would like to get back to that." Another effective statement might be: "Excuse me, but that information is not job-related. Let us get back to your description of a typical day at the office." This is especially appropriate if information being volunteered has the potential for illegal use.

The second possible concern with open-ended questions is that they can be too broad in scope. The classic request, "Tell me about yourself," illustrates this point. Questions that require applicants to summarize many years in a single response are also not effective. An example of this might be, "Describe your work history" when addressing an applicant who has worked for over 30 years. Instead, say, "Please describe your work experience over the past three years." This is still open-ended, but it provides some helpful boundaries.

It is important to note that any question that can be answered by a yes or no can be converted into an open-ended question. For example, "Did you like your last job?" can be changed to, "What did you like about your last job?"

Preemployment inquiries that are considered to be potential EEO violations were listed in Chapter 4. It was noted that the categories of education and experience will provide most of the information needed to make an effective hiring decision without violating any EEO laws. Although each specific position will dictate the most appropriate questions to ask, the following list of inquiries regarding work and education will provide interviewers with a source of effective, legal, open-ended questions from which to choose. Note that it is not necessary to ask all questions in the interrogative form. It can be just as effective to use statements.

Questions Regarding Education

1. What were your favorite and least favorite subjects in high school/college? Why?

2. How were your grades in your favorite and least favorite subjects?
3. What subjects did you do best in? Poorest in?
4. Why did you decide to go to college?
5. Why did you major in _____?
6. Why did you decide to attend _____?
7. What type of extracurricular activities did you participate in? Why did you select those?
8. What career plans did you have at the beginning of college?
9. What career plans did you have when you graduated high school/college?
10. What did you gain by attending high school/college?
11. If you had the opportunity to attend school all over again, what, if anything, would you do differently? Why?
12. What elective courses did you take? Why?
13. How did high school/college prepare you for the "real world"?
14. Describe your studies in the area of _____ (whatever field the job opening is in).
15. How do you feel your studies in the area of _____ have prepared you for this job opening?
16. When did you decide that you wanted to major in _____?
17. Who were your favorite and least favorite teachers in high school/college? Why?
18. Describe your study habits in high school/college.
19. Describe any part-time jobs you had while attending high school/college.
20. Which of your part-time jobs did you find most/least interesting?
21. How did you spend your summers while attending high school/college?
22. Why did you work while attending high school/college?
23. What plans do you have, if any, to continue with school?
24. What did you find to be most difficult about working and attending school at the same time?

25. What advice would you give to someone who wanted to work and attend school simultaneously?

*Questions Relating to Previous Experience and Other
Work-Related Categories*

1. Please describe your activities during at typical day on the job.
2. What is your description of the ideal manager? Subordinate? Co-worker?
3. What kind of people do you find it difficult/easy to work with? Why?
4. What did you like most/least about your last job?
5. What is your description of the ideal work environment?
6. What motivates you? Why?
7. What makes you an effective supervisor?
8. What is the greatest accomplishment of your career to date? Why?
9. Describe a situation at your last job involving pressure. How did you handle it?
10. What do you feel an employer owes an employee?
11. How do you feel about work-related travel?
12. Describe your past experience with work-related travel in terms of duration and frequency.
13. How do you feel about relocation? Are there any places where you would not be willing to relocate?
14. What were some of the duties of your last job that you found to be difficult?
15. How do you feel about the progress that you have made in your career to date?
16. What are some of the problems you encountered in your last job?
17. How does your present job differ from the one you had before it?
18. Of all the jobs you have had, which did you find the most/least rewarding?
19. In what ways do you feel your present job has prepared you to assume additional responsibilities?
20. What has been the most frustrating situation you have encountered in your career to date?

21. Why do you want to leave your present job?
22. How did you feel about the way in which your department/division was managed at your last job?
23. If I were to ask your supervisor to describe your work, what would he or she say?
24. What would you do if . . . ?
25. How would you handle . . . ?
26. What does the prospect of this job offer you that your last job did not?
27. What are you looking for in a company?
28. How does your experience in the military relate to your chosen field?
29. Please describe the work you performed while in the military.
30. What immediate and long term career goals have you set for yourself?
31. What would you like to avoid in future jobs?
32. What are your salary requirements?
33. Who or what has influenced you with regard to your career goals? In what way?
34. To what do you attribute your career success thus far?
35. What do you consider to be your greatest strength?
36. What are the areas in which you require improvement? How would you go about making these improvements?
37. How would you describe yourself as a manager? Subordinate? Co-worker?
38. What aspects of your work give you the greatest satisfaction?
39. How do you approach tasks that you dislike?
40. How do you manage your time?
41. What is your management style?
42. What did you learn from each of your previous jobs?
43. Please give me some examples of decisions you have made on the job. What were the ramifications of these decisions?
44. How do you go about making a decision?
45. How would you describe your delegation skills?
46. How would you describe your standards of performance, both for yourself and for subordinates?

47. How would you describe your relationship with your last supervisor?
48. Please give me an example of a project that did not turn out the way you planned. What happened?
49. Why are you applying for a position with our company?
50. Why did you go to work for your last employer?
51. What is your greatest responsibility at your present job?
52. Describe your progression at your last job.
53. What have past employers complimented/criticized you for?
54. What can you offer our firm?
55. How does this opening fit in with your career objectives?
56. What types of work-related situations make you feel most comfortable/uneasy?
57. Why are you willing to take a reduction in pay?
58. Why did you decide to become a _____?
59. Why do you want to change fields?
60. What is a manager's/employee's greatest responsibility?
61. How do you feel about repetitious tasks?
62. How do you feel about having your work closely supervised?
63. How do you feel about working overtime?
64. How do you feel about being on call?
65. What would motivate you to stay with this company until you are ready to retire?
66. What would make you resign from a position with this company?
67. Under what circumstances, if any, do you feel a supervisor or manager should perform the duties of his or her subordinates?
68. How would you handle an employee who was consistently tardy?
69. This job calls for the ability to _____. What experience have you had in doing this?
70. What is the most difficult/rewarding aspect of being a _____?

71. If you were asked to perform a task that was not in your job description, how would you respond?
72. What is your definition of company loyalty? How far does it extend?
73. How would you go about discussing job dissatisfaction with your boss?
74. What could your previous employer(s) have done to convince you not to leave?
75. If you have ever fired someone, please describe what it was like.
76. Is there anything else I should know about your qualifications that would help me to make a hiring decision?

In addition to these open-ended questions, keep in mind that throughout the interview applicants will be giving you free information upon which you can build more questions. You can also develop more questions by asking the applicant to expand upon or elaborate a response.

HOW TO INTERVIEW PROBLEM APPLICANTS

Most applicants are eager to make a good impression on the interviewer. They try to answer all inquiries as fully as possible, project positive body language, and ask appropriate questions. Occasionally, however, you will find yourself faced with a problem applicant: someone who falls into one of the following categories.

Shy or nervous
Overly talkative
Overly aggressive
Highly emotional or distraught
Dominant (tries to take over the interview)

At the first indication that you are dealing with a problem applicant you must make certain adjustments in your handling of the interview.

1. *Shy or nervous applicants.* Within the first few seconds of the ice-breaker portion of the interview it will become apparent if an applicant is especially shy or nervous. This type of person needs to be drawn out slowly; a broad, open-ended question might be too intimidating if used right off the bat. Instead, try a few close-ended inquiries to put the candidate more at ease. Make them simple, relating to areas with which the applicant is likely to feel comfortable. Also make certain that your first open-ended question pertains to a topic with which the individual has experience, thereby ensuring a certain degree of ease. In addition, try using a softer tone of voice, positive body language, and words of encouragement. Let the applicant know, in every way possible, that you are interested in what he or she has to say.

2. *Overly talkative applicants.* Some candidates seem to be capable of talking nonstop. They not only answer your questions, but volunteer a great deal more information, much of which is irrelevant and unnecessary. These people are often very personable and really quite delightful to talk with. However, you must remind yourself that you are not there to engage in a social conversation. Your goal is to ascertain sufficient information upon which to base a hiring decision.

The key to effectively dealing with applicants who talk too much is control. You must remember that you are in charge of the interview and that you control the amount of time devoted to questions and answers. When you feel that enough data has been gathered, say to the applicant: "Everything you have told me is very interesting. I now have enough information upon which to base my decision. Thank you very much for your time. You will be hearing from us by the end of this week."

Sometimes applicants do not respond to this cue to leave. They remain seated and resume talking. If this occurs, escalate your efforts somewhat. Tell the applicant, "I am afraid that is all the time we have. I do have other applicants waiting." If even this does not work, as a last resort you can add: "I am sure that if you were waiting to see me, you would appreciate my meeting you on time." At this point, if the applicant is still seated, stand up and extend your hand. As you shake hands, gently guide the applicant to the door.

3. *Overly aggressive applicants.* Some applicants present themselves in an overly aggressive or hostile way. Perhaps they have been out of work for a long time, or perhaps they have applied for a job with your company before and were rejected. When confronted with an angry applicant it is important to stay calm and maintain your objectivity. Try to find out why the applicant is so upset. Explain that you cannot continue the interview as long as he or she remains agitated. Try to complete the interview and judge the applicant as fairly as possible, taking into account any extenuating circumstances.

4. *Highly emotional or distraught applicants.* Having an applicant begin to weep in your office can be quite unnerving. If this should occur, extend empathy, not sympathy. You cannot be objective if you become too emotionally involved. Explain to the applicant that he or she must settle down in order for you to continue the interview. Suggest that they leave your office for a few moments to collect themselves. In some rare instances it may be better to reschedule the interview.

5. *Applicants who try to take over the interview.* Sometimes applicants will try to gain control of the interview. This usually happens when someone is trying to cover up for a lack of sufficient job experience. The takeover may occur in a variety of ways, e.g., steering the conversation to the interviewer, discussing books or photos in the room, or going off on a tangent. If this takes place while you are interviewing, all is not lost. Remind yourself that you are in charge and say to the applicant: "Excuse me, but we seem to have strayed, let's get back to . . ."

ONE-ON-ONE VERSUS TEAM INTERVIEWING

Most interviews involve two people: the interviewer and the applicant. Occasionally, however, the team approach may be employed. This involves more than one interviewer—usually two or three. The team may consist of a personnel representative, the department supervisor, and possibly a division head. This is commonly done for one of two reasons: (1) to save the time it would take to schedule two or three separate interviews and (2) to be able to compare impressions of the applicant.

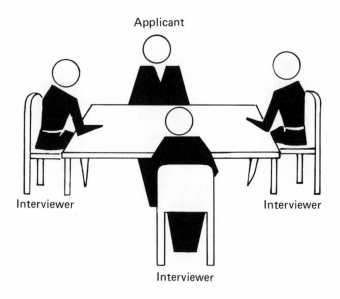

Figure 1.   Surrounding the candidate.

If carefully planned, team interviews can be very effective. The role that each person is going to play should be agreed upon ahead of time. Perhaps the personnel representative will begin by asking some broad questions to determine overall job-suitability; then the department supervisor will ask more detailed, technical questions; finally, the division head will pursue the candidate's potential, and other intangible factors.

Applicants should always be advised ahead of time that the team approach is going to be used. Otherwise, it can be very unnerving to see more than one interviewer in the room. Seating should also be carefully arranged. Unlike a one-on-one interview, where the proximity of the interviewer's chair to the applicant's chair is inconsequential, seating in a team interview situation can create an uncomfortable environment. Do not, for example, surround the candidate's chair. As Figure 1 illustrates, this involves one seat on either side and one seat directly in front of the applicant. This can result in a "tennis match" sort of interview, with the candidate continually turning his or her head

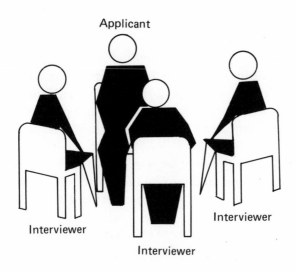

Applicant

Interviewer

Interviewer

Interviewer

Figure 2.   Suggested seating arrangement for a team interview.

from one side to the other, trying to address everyone in the room.

Instead, offer the applicant a seat and form a soft arc in front of him or her. As Figure 2 illustrates, this setting is less structured and more conducive to a productive exchange.

INTERVIEW GUIDELINES AND PITFALLS

With all that has been said thus far about the face-to-face interview it is a good idea to pause at this point and review some important guidelines.

1. *Establish the format.* Make certain that you develop a system that encompasses all of the important ingredients of an interview. Be sure that it reflects your own style and personality.

2. *Establish rapport.* Taking a few moments out at the beginning of an interview to put the applicant at ease will result in a greater exchange of information.

3. *Carefully select your first question.* A well-worded, open-ended question can provide several additional categories for the inteviewer to explore.

4. *Practice active listening skills.* Concentrating closely on what the applicant says and talking no more than 30 percent of the time will enable you to make more effective hiring decisions.

5. *Take notes.* Jot down key words and phrases during the interview and embellish these immediately after the applicant leaves.

6. *Practice positive body language.* Employ those gestures and movements that are likely to be interpreted in an encouraging way. Strive for consistency between verbal statements and non-verbal expressions.

7. *Encourage the applicant to talk.* Repetition, summarization, encouraging phrases, and silence may all be used to encourage applicants to talk.

8. *Consider different types of interview questions.* Virtually every thought can be expressed in six different question forms: Close-ended, open-ended, probing, hypothetical, leading, and loaded. Almost without exception, the open-ended question is the most effective, yielding the most information. Hypothetical questions can also be very productive.

9. *Adjust your approach when dealing with problem applicants.* Shy, nervous, overly aggressive, highly emotional, very talkative, or dominant applicants each require some variation from your regular interviewing approach. Be careful not to become too emotionally involved in these instances—practice empathy, not sympathy. Also be careful not to lose control of the interview.

10. *Plan team interviews carefully.* If carefully planned, the team approach can be very effective. This planning includes the seating arrangement, as well as the role played by each team member.

In addition to these guidelines, there are some pitfalls that interviewers should try to avoid.

1. Avoid interrupting the applicant, as long as he or she is saying something relevant.
2. Avoid agreement or disagreement; instead, express interest and understanding.
3. Avoid using terminology that the applicant is unlikely to be familiar with.
4. Avoid reading the application or resume back to the applicant.
5. Avoid comparisons with the incumbent, previous employees, yourself, or other candidates.
6. Avoid asking unrelated questions together.
7. Avoid talking down to an applicant.
8. Avoid talking about yourself.
9. Avoid hiring an unqualified applicant simply because you are desperate to fill an opening.
10. Avoid trying to duplicate someone else's interviewing style.

CLOSING THE INTERVIEW

Just as some interviewers have trouble knowing how to begin interviews, others are uncertain about how to close them. To help you decide if it is time to end an interview, ask yourself the following questions.

1. Have I asked the applicant enough questions about his or her education and previous experience to determine job-suitability?
2. Have I adequately described the available position and provided sufficient information about this organization?
3. Have I discussed salary, benefits, growth opportunities, and other related topics to the extent that the policy of this company permits?
4. Have I allowed the applicant to ask questions?

If your answers to all four questions are yes, then you are ready to make your closing remarks. These should entail telling the applicant what happens next. For example, you might say:

Well, Ms. Ryan, I believe that I have all the information I need. If I have answered all your questions, I would like to close by telling you what will happen now. We still have a dozen or so more candidates to interview throughout the remainder of this week. After this, we will check references and make our final selection. Everyone will be notified by mail regarding our decision. In the interim, if you have any additional questions, please do not hesitate to call me. I want to thank you for coming in. I have enjoyed talking with you.

SUMMARY

This chapter has described the necessary components of an effective face-to-face employment interview. It began by outlining different interview formats. The importance of establishing rapport was then discussed, followed by some suggestions on how to get into the heart of the interview with the first question. Active listening guidelines were offered, in addition to suggestions for note-taking. The role of body language was described, as were methods for encouraging applicants to talk. Different types of interview questions were assessed and examples of open-ended questions were provided. Techniques for dealing with problem applicants were also noted. The merits and drawbacks of team interviewing were mentioned, followed by a list of interviewing guidelines and pitfalls. Finally, suggestions were offered for effectively closing the interview.

Having concluded the interview, you are now ready to review your impressions of the candidate, and elaborate upon the notes taken during the interview.

6

Writing Up the Interview

In the previous chapter it was suggested that key words and phrases be jotted down throughout the face-to-face interview. It was further suggested that the interviewer elaborate upon these notes immediately after the interview. These notes are a permanent record of your interview, and should be written with care. Whether you use a preprinted form or a blank piece of paper, the same guidelines regarding your notes will apply.

AVOID SUBJECTIVE LANGUAGE

Avoiding subjective language is one of the most important facets of note-taking. All language that is written down must be objective, as opposed to subjective. For example, saying that an applicant is "attractive," is a matter of opinion. On the other hand, if you were to write that "the applicant's appearance is consistent with the employee image desired by the company," that would be objective.

Following are some additional examples of subjective language that should be avoided.

Pretty	Chip on his/her	Ideal candidate
Handsome	shoulder	Lacks luster
Too old	Know-it-all	Needs polish
Too young	Pushy	Too hyper
Cocky	Personable	Sluggish
Arrogant	Warm	No sense of humor
Has a bad attitude	Energetic	Funny

Smart	Cool	Cultured
Refined	Diplomatic	Sarcastic
Manipulative	Tactful	Shrewd
Pompous	Abrasive	Diligent
Pretentious	Boring	Curt
Practical	Reserved	Polished
Vain	Erratic	Narrow-
Distinguished	Eccentric	minded
Somber	Ingenious	Rude
Calculating	Greedy	Careless
Interesting		

These terms can easily bias an interviewer who may be going through the personnel files when trying to fill a future opening.

AVOID RECORDING OPINIONS

Interviewers are cautioned against recording their opinions. The following expressions will illustrate this point.

1. I feel Ms. Jenkins would make an excellent supervisor.
2. I believe Mr. Curtis is the perfect candidate for this job.
3. I think Mr. Turner will make a good mechanic.
4. I consider Ms. Hastings to be excellent secretarial material.
5. I am of the opinion that Mr. Valentine will make a very good accountant.
6. It is my view that Ms. Heller will do quite well as a data processing operator.
7. As I see it, Mr. Murphy is just right for this job.
8. To my way of thinking, Ms. Windsor will make a great telephone operator.
9. If you ask me, we have found our next assistant vice president in Ms. Martin.

10. In my judgment, Mr. Princeton will make an excellent project coordinator.
11. Mr. Casper seems to be the best administrative applicant we have seen.
12. Ms. Davis appears to be perfect for the office assistant position.

These broad, subjective, summarizing statements do not refer to anything factual. If anyone other than the original interviewer were to read these notes, they would not be able to determine the applicant's job-suitability.

REFER TO JOB-RELATED FACTS

Using the job description as a guide will ensure the writing of only job-related facts. In addition, it will preclude the possibility of noting any information that might violate EEO laws. There are two excellent techniques that can be employed in this regard: (1) referring directly to each of the position's duties and requirements and then indicating whether or not the applicant has the necessary experience or skills; and (2) recording direct quotes as they are made by the applicant.

Consider this example. You are trying to fill the position of secretary to the president of your organization. Here are the primary duties and responsibilities of the job, taken from the job description.

1. Takes, transcribes, and edits dictation. Dictation may be taken directly, over the phone, or from a machine. Editing of dictation includes research for the completion of correspondence and/or reports involved.
2. Schedules all appointments and meetings for the president. Arranges the president's travel itinerary, including commutation, reservations, and accommodations.
3. Screens all calls and visitors to the president's office.
4. Opens, reroutes and disposes of all correspondence directed to the president.

5. Replies to routine inquiries.
6. Supervises record and filing system of all correspondence and reports in the president's office, including confidential information.
7. Delegates routine typing and filing to clerk-typists and supervises work of same.
8. Prepares and writes formal minutes of all board meetings, and shareholder and executive committee meetings as well.
9. Prepares various reports required for meetings of the board of directors, shareholders, and executive committee.
10. Performs other related secretarial duties as required.

As you interview each candidate applying for this position, refer to the specific job requirements. A partial sample interview might go something like this:

Interviewer: "Please describe the extent of your experience taking dictation over the past three years in your present position as senior secretary."

Applicant: "Well, my boss, who is a vice president, dictates by machine about three times a week. Sometimes she dictates directly to me and I take down everything in shorthand and then transcribe it."

Interviewer: "How much research does this involve?"

Applicant: "None. I just type what she says."

Interviewer: "What are your responsibilities with regard to scheduling appointments and meetings?"

Applicant: "Oh, I do all of that. I even arrange international trips, because my boss travels to Europe about a half-dozen times a year. It's up to me to book her hotel reservations and everything like that."

Interviewer: "What do you do when someone calls or stops by your office and wants to speak with or see your boss?"

Applicant: "By now, I pretty much know who she wants to see and who I should turn away. I use my judgment and may tell someone she's in a meeting and cannot be disturbed. I will also offer my help. Sometimes the person has a question that I can answer."

Interviewer: "What happens if someone insists, saying it is urgent?"

Applicant: "I repeat myself, saying she is in a meeting, and again, offer to help. I try to be polite and professional at all times, even though some people can get pretty nasty."

Interviewer: "What are your responsibilities with regard to the mail?"

Applicant: "I open all the mail, except envelopes marked 'confidential.' Then I stamp everything and put the pile on my boss's desk. She likes to go through everything herself."

Interviewer: "Then what happens?"

Applicant: "Then, about mid-morning, she returns those letters, memos, and reports requiring action. She attaches little notes to everything, telling me who to call or what to type."

Interviewer: "What is the extent of any supervisory responsibility you may have?"

Applicant: "I don't have any. I do everything myself."

Interviewer: "Am I correct in understanding, then, that you do not delegate any typing or filing to anyone else?"

Applicant: "That's correct. I do it all myself. My boss gives some typing and filing to a clerk-typist in the office, but I don't get involved with that."

Interviewer: "What about taking minutes at meetings?"

Applicant: "No, I don't do that. The president's secretary does it."

Interviewer: "What kind of things do you type on a regular basis?"

Applicant: "The usual: letters, memos; that kind of thing."

Interviewer: "What about things you type less frequently?"

Applicant: "I type a monthly project status report and then a quarterly report."

Interviewer: "What is the quarterly report about?"

Applicant: "It includes quarterly accomplishments and the goals for the next quarter."

Interviewer: "What other secretarial duties do you perform?"

Applicant: "I also type our department's budget."

Interviewer: "How frequently does that occur?"
Applicant: "Only twice a year, but it takes a long time to do."

This partial interview illustrates the importance of writing down job-related facts as they relate to the duties and requirements of a job. The interviewer related each question to one of the responsibilities listed in the job description. As the applicant responded, the interviewer might have jotted down the following key words and phrases.

> V.P.
> Dictate: three times per week (mach/direct)
> No research
> Appt's, meetgs, travel (internat)
> See/call: judgment; offer help; "polite and profess at all
>   times"
> All mail—not confid; stamp only
> No super/delegat
> No minutes
> Memos, letters, reports
> Typ annual budget

After the applicant has gone the interviewer can review these thoughts and elaborate on his or her notes. By once again referring to the position's requirements, he or she can determine overall job-suitability. The final set of notes, based on this portion of the interview, might read like this:

Applicant has worked as secretary to V.P. for three years. Regular responsibilities include: dictation (by machine and shorthand); scheduling appointments, meetings, and making travel arrangements (domestic and international); opening and stamping mail; typing memos, letters, and reports; and screening calls and visitors. When asked how she would handle persistent callers, she responded, "I try to be polite and professional at all times." Also types annual budget. Lacks experience with research, supervision, delegation, and taking minutes.

Everything written is a job-related fact, including the

quote, which reflects an intangible quality that is important in this position.

BE DESCRIPTIVE

Some interviewers conduct volume interviews; that is, they schedule perhaps 40 or more interviews a week. After seeing so many people it is difficult to refer back to each person's application or resume and differentiate them from one another. Even notes that are objective, factual, and job-related may not succeed in jogging your recollection of a specific candidate. To help you with this, consider the occasional use of descriptive phrases. Their purpose is limited to identifying the person and helping you recall the specific interview. Care must be taken in the use of such phrases for two primary reasons: first, they can easily become subjective; and second, even though factual, they are not job-related. To illustrate, "Applicant was dressed entirely in yellow" is an objective descriptive phrase. The addition of just one word, however, could make it subjective: "Applicant was garishly dressed entirely in yellow."

Here are some additional examples of objective description.

Smiled during the entire 30 minutes of the interview
Hair extended below waist
Wore blue nail polish
Wore pearl cuff links
Chain-smoked throughout entire 90 minutes of the interview
Twirled hair
Played with paper clips
Tapped fingers
Taller than 6' 6" (doorway to office is 6' 6")
Laughed frequently
Chewed gum
Rocked in chair

Interviewers are cautioned against using any of these descriptive terms in the selection process. They are only intended to help you remember the applicant, not to decide on job-suitability.

TAPE RECORDING INTERVIEWS

Some interviewers feel that there are too many problems re-lating to note-taking, including the amount of time it takes and the possibility of writing something down that violates EEO regulations. Instead of following the simple rules just cited, they reason that it is easier to tape record the entire interview. Of course, it is difficult to refute the fact that it's easier to record then to write. However, there are two very good reasons for not doing this.

1. If the applicant knows that you are recording the inter-view, this is almost guaranteed to make him or her feel nervous and reluctant to speak freely. It also causes some candidates to become angry and defensive.

2. If the applicant does not know that you are recording the interview, you are violating his or her right to privacy.

The only time that a tape recorder can reasonably be used as part of the employment process is after an interview is com-pleted; the interviewer may then choose to record his or her observations before the next scheduled candidate arrives. Even if this is done however, the interviewer should transfer the dic-tated thoughts to paper; written notes should accompany every application or resume.

ASSIGNING NUMERICAL VALUES

Some organizations incorporate a point system in the note-tak-ing stage of the interview. When using this method the inter-viewer assigns a numerical value to each factor evaluated. Fac-tors appear on a preprinted form with a key that briefly explains the point value of each rating. For example, the overall rating for a five-point value system might look like this:

1. Superior overall skills and qualifications
2. Above average skills and qualifications
3. Meets the requirements of the job
4. Fails to meet all of the requirements of the job
5. Not qualified

Then, each individual factor might be evaluated according to the following scale.

1. Outstanding
2. Very good
3. Good
4. Fair
5. Poor

There are a number of problems with this kind of system.

1. The accompanying point value form may contain factors that are subjective and are not job-related. These may include appearance, personality, awareness, maturity, tact, and self-confidence.

2. As explained earlier, using subjective terms such as *outstanding* or *poor* to judge someone is meaningless.

3. Busy interviewers who rely on forms with several pre-printed categories tend to quickly check off boxes without giving enough thought to each person's actual skill level.

4. Without specific written details regarding each applicant, it will be extremely difficult to distinguish one person from another at a later date.

If forms are used, they should include only job-related factors, (i.e., education and experience). In addition, ample space should be allowed for the interviewer's notes. Evaluation categories of "meets job requirements" and "fails to meet job requirements" may be included as well. A sample interview evaluation form appears in Appendix G.

Of course, a form does not have to be used at all; a blank space left at the bottom of the application, or a blank piece of paper attached to the application or resume will suffice. Just remember to restrict your comments to objective, factual, and job-related information.

NO REQUIREMENTS AND NO EXPERIENCE

You may find yourself recruiting for jobs that do not carry any experiential or educational requirements. These are usually entry-level positions or jobs requiring very simple, repetitive tasks. Naturally, when this occurs you cannot evaluate someone's demonstrated skill level. In these instances, consider posing hypothetical questions relative to the specific tasks of the job and recording the applicant's reply. For instance, suppose that the opening for a messenger calls for picking up presorted mail from the mail room and distributing it to each employee. During the course of the interview, you might ask an applicant: "What would you do if an employee told you that he or she was expecting a very important letter, but it wasn't included in the mail you had just brought to him or her?" The applicant might reply:"I would give that person the name and extension of my supervisor to check on it." Your notes for this interview might then include the following reference to this job-related activity: "When asked how would handle missing mail, said, 'Tell employee to check with supervisor.'"

EFFECTIVE AND INEFFECTIVE NOTES

At this time it will be helpful to illustrate both effective and ineffective note-taking. An abridged job description for the position of personnel assistant, and excerpts from an interview for this position will be presented for your consideration. It should be noted that the interview excerpts only include questions asked by the interviewer. They do not include detailed information provided about the job and the company, nor do they include questions asked by the applicant. Following the interview excerpts are examples of effective and ineffective note-taking.

Job Description for Personnel Assistant

Duties and Responsibilities

Primary Duties and Responsibilities include:

1. Recruits applicants for nonexempt level positions.
2. Interviews and screens all applicants for nonexempt positions; refers qualified candidates to appropriate department manager/supervisor.
3. Assists department manager/supervisor with hiring decisions.
4. Performs reference checks on potential employees, by telephone and in writing.
5. Processes new employees in terms of payroll and benefits; informs new employees of all pertinent information.
6. Responsible for conveying all necessary insurance information to employees and assisting them with questions, processing of claims, etcetera.
7. Assists in the implementation of policies and procedures; may explain or interpret certain policies as required.
8. Assists in the maintenance and administration of company's wage and salary administration program; monitors salary increase recommendations as they are received to ensure compliance with merit increase guidelines.
9. Advises managers/supervisors of employee performance review schedule; follows up on delinquent or inconsistent reviews.
10. Responsible for the orderly and systematic maintenance of all employee records and files.
11. Assists EEO officer with advising managers/supervisors on matters of equal employment opportunity and affirmative action as they pertain to the interviewing and hiring process and employer-employee relations.

12. Assists in the maintenance of up-to-date job descriptions of positions throughout the company.
13. Maintains all necessary personnel records and reports; this includes unemployment insurance reports, flow-log recording, EEO reports, change notices, and identification card records.
14. Conducts exit interviews for terminating nonexempt employees.
15. Assists personnel manager and personnel director with the planning and conducting of each month's organizational orientation program.
16. Performs other related duties and assignments as required.

Prior Experience and/or Education

Thorough general knowledge and understanding of the personnel function; prior experience as a nonexempt interviewer, preferably in a manufacturing environment; ability to work effectively with all levels of management and large numbers of employees; ability to deal effectively with applicants and referral sources.

Partial Interview for Personnel Assistant

Interviewer: "Good morning, Ms. Oliver. Thank you for coming in. Please be seated."
Applicant: "Thank you. I'm glad to be here and, by the way, it's *Mrs.* Oliver, but you can call me Sandra."
Interviewer: "Did you have any difficulty getting here, Sandra?"
Applicant: "No, my daughter attends nursery school about one mile from here, so I'm very familiar with the area."
Interviewer: "Well, I'm glad that you didn't have any trouble. I'm anxious to begin talking with you about your interests in our opening for a personnel assistant."
Applicant: "Oh, I'm ready! I've been looking forward to this all week. I really want this job!"
Interviewer: "Fine. Then why don't we begin to discuss

your qualifications as they relate to the responsibilities of this job."

Applicant: "Great!"

Interviewer: "To begin with, the job requires recruiting, interviewing, and screening applicants for all of our non-exempt positions. Please describe your experience in this regard."

Applicant: "Well, that's exactly what I've been doing for the past year at Circuits, Inc."

Interviewer: "Please explain what you mean."

Applicant: "Well, whenever I receive an approved job requisition, it's up to me to start recruiting. The first thing I do is talk with department heads to make sure that I understand the requirements and duties of the job. I also try to visit the department in order to get a feel for the work environment and to see first-hand what the person will be doing. It also helps beef up my rapport with the department head. Let's see; where was I? Oh, yes; then I start to explore different recruitment sources."

Interviewer: "Such as?"

Applicant: "The usual: agencies, want-ads, walk-ins, employee referrals."

Interviewer: "Any others?"

Applicant: "That's usually all it takes. We don't have any trouble attracting applicants. We have a fine reputation in the manufacturing industry, as I'm sure you know."

Interviewer: "Please, continue."

Applicant: "Well, I interview and screen all the applicants, and then refer those qualified to the department head."

Interviewer: "Where did you learn to interview?"

Applicant: "I have a degree in personnel administration, as you can see on my resume, and then I received on-the-job training when I first joined Circuits, Inc."

Interviewer: "How much time was devoted to on-the-job training?"

Applicant: "About three months; then I was left on my own."

Interviewer: "I see. Please, go on."

Applicant: "Okay. As I said, I refer qualified candidates to the department head. Then, we get together and decide on who to hire."

Interviewer: "Who finally makes the actual hiring decision?"

Applicant: "The department heads and I usually agree, but if we disagree, they decide. After all, they're the ones who have to work with the person."

Interviewer: "What are your responsibilities with regard to reference checks?"

Applicant: "I run both written and telephone references on only those applicants we're interested in."

Interviewer: "Once the applicant is selected, what do you do?"

Applicant: "I arrange the starting date and schedule them for orientation. It's also my job to put them on payroll and take care of their benefits."

Interviewer: "So then, it is your responsibility to explain all of the company benefits?"

Applicant: "No, not exactly. I just process the paperwork. Someone from the benefits department explains all of that during orientation."

Interviewer: "I understand. Tell me, Sandra, does Circuits, Inc. have a policies and procedure manual?"

Applicant: "Yes, it does."

Interviewer: "What are your responsibilities with regard to this manual?"

Applicant: "Sometimes if my boss, the personnel manager, is not around, I try to answer questions from department heads, but I don't usually get involved with that."

Interviewer: "In addition to recruiting, interviewing, screening, and processing payroll and benefits paperwork, what other areas of personnel are you involved with?"

Applicant: "Well, let's see. Let me think for a minute. Oh yes, I'm in charge of performance reviews."

Interviewer: "In what way are you in charge of performance reviews?"

Applicant: "I keep a log of when each nonexempt employee's review is due and notify the department head if they don't get them in on time."

Interviewer: "I see. Is there anything else, say with regard to salary administration?"

Applicant: "We have a wage and salary manager who takes care of that."

Interviewer: "What about EEO and affirmative action?"

Applicant: "No. Our EEO officer handles that. I know a lot about those areas though."

Interviewer: "You know alot about EEO and affirmative action?"

Applicant: "Yes. I studied it in school and attended a three-day seminar on it about six months ago. I'd like to specialize in EEO some day."

Interviewer: "What other personnel responsibilities do you have as a personnel assistant at Circuits, Inc.?"

Applicant: "Well, I help with job descriptions."

Interviewer: "In what way?"

Applicant: "Whenever there's a nonexempt job opening, I check with the department head to make sure that the job has not changed significantly and that the existing job description is still valid. If it needs revamping, I tell my boss and she takes over from there."

Interviewer: "What are your responsibilities with regard to personnel files and records?"

Applicant: "I keep an applicant flow-log and process employment change notices."

Interviewer: "Any other forms?"

Applicant: "None that I can think of."

Interviewer: "What about any involvement with exit interviews?"

Applicant: "Oh, yes, I forgot about that! I do all exit interviews for nonexempt employees. I enjoy that!"

Interviewer: "What is it that you enjoy about it?"

Applicant: "I like finding out why a person is leaving and what the company might do in the future to prevent good people from leaving."

Interviewer: "I see. That's very interesting."

Applicant: "Yes. I really like that part of my job."

Interviewer: "What other aspects of your work do you enjoy?"

Applicant: "I like the interviewing: you know, talking to so many different people."

Interviewer: "What don't you like about your job, Sandra?"

Applicant: "If I had to pick one thing, I guess it would be the paperwork: mostly the employment change notices."

Interviewer: "What aspect of your job do you find to be the most difficult?"

Applicant: "I guess that would be my part in the monthly orientation program."

Interviewer: "You participate in the orientation program?"

Applicant: "Yes, didn't I mention that? I have to give an opening talk of about 20 minutes about the history of Circuits, Inc.; why it's such a great place to work; that sort of thing."

Interviewer: "What is it about doing this that you find difficult?"

Applicant: "I get nervous talking in front of people."

Interviewer: "I see. Sandra, I'd like to get back for a moment to your educational training in personnel administration. What made you decide to pursue this field?"

Applicant: "It seemed challenging and varied. It also seemed to offer a lot in the way of growth opportunities."

Interviewer: "What level do you ultimately want to achieve?"

Applicant: "I think I'd like to be a EEO officer."

Interviewer: "What were your grades like in college, both in personnel courses and in other courses?"

Applicant: "I graduated with a 3.0 average. I did pretty well in everything except math. I failed statistics."

Interviewer: "What did your personnel courses consist of?"

Applicant: "Everything: The degree prepared us to be generalists."

Interviewer: "I know you said that you particularly like EEO. What aspects of personnel do you enjoy the least?"

Applicant: "That would have to be benefits. I really find it kind of dry and boring."

Interviewer: "I understand. Sandra, I have just a few more questions to ask you. Tell me, what would you do if an applicant acted up? By that I mean, became aggressive or cried."

Applicant: "I'd try to calm them down. That's happened a few times to me and after a few minutes they usually settled down."

Interviewer: "What did you say to make the applicant settle down?"

Applicant: "I told them that I wanted to learn about their qualifications, but that I couldn't do so if they didn't stop shouting or whatever it was they were doing. It worked."

Interviewer: "How did that make you feel?"

Applicant: "I felt bad for them. I could see how much they wanted the job. But I also knew I had to remain objective if I was going to evaluate them fairly."

Interviewer: "What does the prospect of this job offer you that your present job does not?"

Applicant: "It's time for a change."

Interviewer: "A change?"

Applicant: "Yes. One year in Circuits, Inc. is long enough. It's not the most exciting place in the world to work."

Interviewer: "What is your idea of an ideal work environment?"

Applicant: "One where employees who prove themselves can grow; also, where managers don't look over your shoulder all the time. Of course, I would like to be paid more, too!"

Interviewer: "What type of employee are you?"

Applicant: "I like to work independently. I don't need close supervision."

Interviewer: "What do you feel you could offer our firm?"

Applicant: "I'm a hard worker and I love personnel."

Interviewer: "Is there anything else I should know about your qualifications that would help me to make a hiring decision?"

Applicant: "I can't think of anything else."

Interviewer: "Fine, Sandra, I'd like to thank you again for coming in. We will be interviewing for the next ten days or so, and will make our decision at the end of that time. All applicants will be notified by mail. If you have any questions in the interim, please do not hesitate to call me. I've enjoyed talking with you."

Applicant: "Thank you. I've enjoyed talking with you, too. I really want this job!"

Interviewer: "I understand. Good-bye, Sandra."

Applicant: "Good-bye."

Examples of Ineffective Notes

Here are the ineffective notes taken as a result of the interview.

Married; young daughter
Too anxious
Tends to ramble
Only nine months real experience; degree okay
Likes P&P involvement
Had trouble remembering what else she does
Interested in EEO; I smell trouble
No real J.D. experience
Light recordkeeping
Sounds like a troublemaker; loves to find out why people
    leave the company, then tries to get company to make
    changes
Dislikes doing orientation
Dislikes benefits
Light experience with problem applicants
Bored with present job
Wants more money and to move up
Doesn't like supervision

Summarizing statement: "I don't feel Mrs. Oliver would make a very good personnel assistant. She just doesn't seem reliable. Also, she hasn't demonstrated a thorough knowledge of personnel."

As you can see, these statements are highly subjective. In addition, many of the comments are not job-related.

Examples of Effective Notes

Now, let us review the effective notes.

Circuits, Inc., manufacturing

Nonexempt interviewing experience—9 months; 3 months O.J.T.;

Degree in personnel admin

Recruits, interviews (enjoys), screens, and recommends for hire

Telephone and written references

Processes payroll and benefits paperwork

P&P manual; most questions handled by personnel manager (boss)

No sal. admin. responsibility

Expressed interest in pursuing field of EEO

Checks on accuracy of existing J.D.s

Flow-log and employee change notices (enjoys least)

Exit interviews for all nonexempt employees (enjoys)

Participates in monthly orientation program: "nervous talking in front of people"

Least favorite: benefits

Reason for leaving: "time for a change"

Has dealt with applicants who have acted up; knew it was important to remain objective

"Like to work independently"

"I'm a hard worker; I love personnel"

Summarizing statement: "This job calls for a thorough general knowledge and understanding of personnel and prior experience as a nonexempt interviewer. Ms. Oliver has had three months on-the-job training and nine months actual experience in the following areas of personnel at Circuits, Inc.: nonexempt recruitment; interviewing; screening; references; processing payroll and benefits paperwork; checking accuracy of job descriptions; flow-logs and employee change notices; exit interviews; monthly orientation. Also has a degree in personnel administration. Recommends hiring; interested in EEO; enjoys exit interviews; least favorite—benefits. 'Wants a change';

'Likes to work independently'; 'hard worker'; 'loves personnel.'"

These statements are all objective, factual, and job-related. Anyone reading them would have an immediate understanding of the applicant's skill level as it relates to the requirements of the job.

SUMMARY

This chapter examined the four main ingredients of effective interview note-taking. In summary, they are as follows.

Avoid subjective language
Avoid recording opinions
Refer to job-related facts
Be descriptive

In addition, the problems of using a numerical value or point system were examined. Suggestions were offered regarding notes for jobs without educational or experiential requirements. Finally, examples of effective and ineffective notes were provided.

With carefully written notes, you can now proceed to select the best possible candidate for the job.

7

Making the Selection

After having screened and interviewed all the applicants for a job, it is time to make your selection. Many interviewers find this the most difficult step in the employment process, since several candidates may possess the required qualifications.

REFERENCES

Begin the final selection process by checking the references of the candidates being considered. Usually there will be two or three candidates who have impressed you with their overall job-suitability. In checking their references, focus on contacting previous employers. Depending on the requirements of the job, you may also want to verify educational credentials. Although personal references almost never have any merit, they may occasionally be needed to supplement other character or professional references.

Before examining these different types of references, it is important to consider the following guidelines.

1. Conduct all reference checks in a uniform manner. That is to say, never single out only women or minorities for reference checks. Inconsistency may be viewed as discriminatory.
2. If an applicant is rejected because of a negative recommendation, be prepared to document the job-related reason.
3. If while doing a reference check, you discover that an applicant has filed an EEO charge, it is illegal to refuse to hire that person because of this.

4. The application form should contain language whereby applicants grant you permission to contact their former employers.
5. Carefully question the validity of comments made by former employers. It is not uncommon for employers to express negative feelings toward a good employee who resigned for a better position. Likewise, employees terminated for poor performance sometimes work out a deal with their former employers, ensuring them of positive reference checks. Therefore, probe for objective statements regarding job performance.
6. Exercise caution when interpreting a respondent's tone of voice, or use of silence and implication.
7. Applicants should be given the opportunity to refute negative references.
8. The Family Education Rights and Privacy Act (Buckley Amendment) allows students to inspect their scholastic records and to prevent a school from releasing certain information without permission.
9. If possible, check with a minimum of two previous employers in order to rule out the possibility of either positive or negative bias. This may also help you to become aware of patterns in an individual's work habits.
10. Reference checks should be conducted by the person who interviewed the applicant. If the interview was conducted by representatives from both personnel and the department in which the opening exists, the personnel specialist usually does the reference checks.
11. Do not automatically assume that a reported personality clash is the applicant's fault.
12. Having been fired does not necessarily mean that a person is a bad risk. People are terminated for many reasons; get an explanation before jumping to conclusions.

Employment References

Employment references are commonly checked by mail or phone. In rare instances, for example, with some executive level positions, they may be pursued in person. This is extremely time-consuming, however, and often completely impractical (e.g., when a former employer is in another part of the country).

Let us first examine *employment references conducted by mail.* Written references usually employ form letters that are designed to verify facts provided by the applicant. Unless directed to the attention of a specific supervisor or department head, these forms are often completed by personnel clerks who rely on the former employee's file for information. Even when addressed to the applicant's former manager, these inquiries may be routinely turned over to the company's personnel department for response. This is because of the increased number of lawsuits resulting from reference-related matters. Indeed, many employers hesitate to provide any unfavorable information and many will only confirm the person's job title, dates of employment, and company's policy regarding eligibility for rehire. Therefore, a true picture of the candidate's skill level is not ascertained.

Another drawback to a written reference is the amount of time it takes to receive a response. Even if the request is marked "Rush," it generally takes a minimum of one to two weeks for a reply. This is valuable time lost if you are waiting for the reference to be returned before making a hiring decision. In fact, the person you finally select may have accepted another job offer in the interim.

For these reasons, it is usually not desirable to conduct a written reference check. Unfortunately, however, some organizations will not provide you with information in any other way. If this is the case, make certain that your written request is comprehensive, but not too time-consuming. Each question should be straight-forward, easy to understand, and work-related. It is also advisable to have two separate form letters: one for exempt employees and another for nonexempt employees. In addition, try to direct your request to the applicant's former supervisor. You may also want to call this person prior to sending the letter. This way, you can make certain that he or she is still employed with the company and in addition, you can stress the importance of a speedy reply. A follow-up phone call approximately three to four days after your request has been mailed may also help to expedite a reply.

Telephone reference checks are a more useful means for achieving information regarding an applicant's experience. They take far less time to conduct and are likely to yield more information.

Conducting telephone reference checks is much like conducting an interview. Virtually all the same skills (e.g., active listening and encouraging the other person to talk) are employed. In fact, just about the only facet of an employment interview that cannot be incorporated into a telephone reference check is body language. Since it is so similar to an interview, preparation for a telephone reference check plays a key role. Begin by deciding who to call. Ask the applicant for the names of his or her immediate supervisor and anyone else who is qualified to comment on the quality of his or her work. Also ascertain the name of someone you may contact in the human resource department. It may be necessary to speak with more than one person: the supervisor and others with whom the applicant directly worked will be able to discuss work performance; personnel will provide information regarding such matters as job title, dates of employment, absenteeism, tardiness, and salary history.

It is also important to prepare a phone-reference form in advance. As with a written reference form, you may want to have one for exempt positions and one for nonexempt positions. The same form can actually be used for both written and phone references. However, in designing the forms, keep in mind that phone references will yield more information and therefore, will require more space for your notes. It is also likely that you will ask some questions in addition to those on the form. Therefore, allow ample room between questions to take notes. A sample reference form for exempt positions is provided in Appendix H, and a sample form for nonexempt positions is found in Appendix I.

When conducting a telephone reference check, first identify yourself, your organization, and the reason for your call. To illustrate: "Good morning, Mr. White. My name is Peter Fisher. I am the personnel representative for XYZ, Inc., and I am conducting a reference check on your former employee, Ms. Susan Downey."

If there is any reluctance on the part of the previous employer, offer your phone number and suggest that he or she call you to verify your identity. If it is a long distance call, offer to receive the call collect.

Always begin by verifying the information provided by the applicant. This will help the former employer recall specific information about the individual. For example, you might say, "Ms. Downey has informed me that she worked for you in the payroll department as a clerk-typist, from June, 1982 through April, 1984. She indicated that she typed various letters, memos, and reports, and was also in charge of the department's filing. Is this correct?"

While listening to your opening statement, the respondent's thought speed will enable him or her to think about other facts regarding this person's work. At this point you will be able to proceed with the other categories on your reference form. As soon as you feel that the former employer is willing to volunteer information, shift from close-ended questions to open-ended questions.

There is one other point that should be made regarding employment reference checks. This involves contacting an applicant's present employer. This can be particularly important if the candidate has only had one job. Understandably, most people will not grant permission to contact their present employer, for fear of jeopardizing their job. How then, can this situation be resolved to the satisfaction of everyone involved? If it is decided, based on the other factors evaluated in the selection process, that this person is the candidate best suited for the position, you can extend the job offer contingent upon receiving a satisfactory reference from his or her employer. Ask to be notified as soon as he or she resigns, and then proceed to conduct a reference check.

Educational References

As previously stated, applicants must provide written consent before a school may release educational records to a prospective employer. A space for this permission may appear on the application form, or a separate release form may be used. Once the proper release has been obtained, academic information may be ascertained, normally for a small fee.

Be certain to include the following categories when checking on educational credentials.

Dates attended
Major
Minor
Courses relevant to the position applied for
Degree received
Honors received
Attendance record
Work-study program participation
Grade averages

In considering this last point, remember that the value of scholastic achievement varies from school to school. An overall index of 3.5 in one college might be equivalent to an index of 2.8 in another. Therefore, it is important to know something about the standing and reputation of a particular school.

Also be careful about drawing conclusions based on grades. Not everyone does well on tests or in a classroom setting. This does not mean, however, that they have not gained the knowledge needed to perform a particular job. Likewise, outstanding grades do not, in and of themselves, mean that someone will excel in a position.

Educational references are generally most useful in confirming the validity of information provided by an applicant. This can be important, as applicants have been known to falsely claim to possess degrees. Educational references may also prove to be valuable when an applicant has had little or no previous work experience. Remember, however, that these references should only be conducted when a job description clearly calls for specific educational achievements.

Personal References

Many application forms still ask candidates to provide names of personal references. Usually, three names are called for, along with titles, phone numbers, and addresses. Some interviewers claim that the type of person used as a reference is significant; that is, whether the person is a doctor or a lawyer or a teacher or whatever. Still others contact the people listed and ask them for the names of additional references.

Personal references generally, prove to be useless. They should be avoided unless interviewers have absolutely no other source of employment or educational information to check.

FACTORS TO CONSIDER

In addition to checking references, there are additional factors to consider before making the final selection.

1. Review your objectives.
2. Reread the job description to ensure thorough familiarity with the concrete requirements, duties, and responsibilities of the position.
3. Review the work history and relevant educational credentials of each candidate.
4. Consider the intangible requirements of the job.
5. Evaluate applicants' reactions to various matters, (e.g., those relating to the position's work environment).
6. Recall and evaluate each applicant's body language.
7. Take each applicant's salary requirements into consideration with regard to the salary range for the position.
8. Assess reasons offered for leaving previous employers.
9. Consider the applicant's potential, especially if the opening is a stepping-stone to other positions.

Going through these nine steps often reveals information which slightly favors one applicant over the others under final consideration. Also remember to take into account your organization's affirmative action goals and their role in the selection process, as described in Chapter 4.

WHO SHOULD CHOOSE

Reviewing the results of reference checks, going through the steps just outlined, and considering your affirmative action goals should ideally be done by everyone who participated in the interviewing process. This usually means a member of the human resource department and one or more representatives from the unit where the opening exists. These individuals should meet, sharing their views regarding the candidates under consideration. A summary sheet identifying the concrete and intangible requirements of the job may be prepared for each applicant so that qualifications can be easily compared. In most instances, an assessment of all the data collected will point in the direction of one candidate and everyone concerned will agree as to who will make the best employee. Occasionally, however, the departmental representative will favor one person and the personnel specialist will prefer another. If after listening to each other's reasons there is still disagreement, then the departmental representative should make the final selection. After all, he or she is the one who will be working directly with the employee on a day-to-day basis.

NOTIFYING THE CHOSEN CANDIDATE

Upon making a hiring decision, many interviewers immediately send letters to those candidates who were not chosen. This is a mistake. Letters of rejection should not go out until the chosen applicant has been offered the job and accepted the offer. This is important. You may have decided to hire someone who has already accepted another position. Or perhaps the exact starting salary offered may not be deemed acceptable. Therefore, you may have to select someone else. It is extremely awkward to approach your second choice after having just sent him or her a letter of rejection.

Offers for all jobs should be in writing. This can be done after a verbal offer has been made and accepted. Details regarding such matters as starting date and preemployment physicals are also worked out by phone. With most exempt level positions, both the offer and the acceptance is confirmed in writing. Letters are usually sent by the personnel specialist with copies to all department representatives concerned. It is extremely important that the content be concise and accurate, with

October 8, 1986

Ms. Elizabeth Downey
55 Poplar Street
Plainfield, New Jersey 07060

Dear Ms. Downey:

We are pleased to confirm our offer for the position of clerk-typist in the payroll department of XYZ, Inc. at a starting salary of $350.00 per week. As discussed, you will begin work at 9:00 A.M. on Monday, November 4, 1985. At that time, please report to Ms. Taylor, the payroll supervisor, in room 219 on the second floor of our building, located at the address noted above.

The nursing office has been apprised of your starting date and will be expecting you for your preemployment physical anytime before that date, Monday through Friday, between 9:00 A.M. and 12:00 noon.

As agreed, you will resign from your present position upon receipt of this job offer. Upon doing so, please notify this office so that we may conduct a reference check. It is understood that this job offer is contingent upon receiving a satisfactory reference from your present employer.

Enclosed is a benefits package describing your health and life insurance options, as well as other company benefits. Also enclosed is our employee handbook for your review. Please bring both items with you when you begin work on November 4. There will be an orientation program scheduled for later that morning, during which time these and other matters will be discussed. *(continues)*

If you have any questions, please do not hesitate to call me at (212) 495-2200, extention 442.

We look forward to having you join our organization.

Sincerely,

Peter Fisher
Personnel Representative

PF/ed

Figure 3.   Sample letter confirming a job offer.

no room for misunderstanding. The following elements should be included.

Official job title
Department and division in which the position exists
Starting salary
Starting date
Time to report to work
Location
Person to see
Arrangements made regarding a preemployment physical
Agreement made regarding a reference check with the
     present employer
Identification of any literature enclosed
Who to contact with questions

The sample letter shown in Figure 3 incorporates these elements.

REJECTION LETTERS

Once a candidate has been selected and your job offer has been accepted it is time to notify the other applicants. Rejection letters

October 8, 1986

Ms. Mary Parker
128 Field Avenue
Union, New Jersey 07083

Dear Ms. Parker:

Thank you for meeting with us to discuss the position of project coordinator in the Management Information Services department of XYZ, Inc.

We found your background and skills to be impressive. However, after a careful evaluation of all factors, we have selected another candidate whose qualifications are more suitable to our requirements.

Your resume will be kept on file and we will contact you if a position that more nearly matches your abilities becomes available.

We wish you the best of luck in your future endeavors.

Sincerely,

Peter Fisher
Personnel Representative

PF/ed

Figure 4. Sample rejection letter.

should refer to the specific position for which an individual applied. In other words, do not reject the person overall; you may want to consider him or her for another position in the future.

The tone of your letter should be professional and sincere. Without going into detail, a statement as to why another candidate has been accepted should be included. This is far more desirable than saying that the person was found unacceptable.

Rejection letters should also be fairly brief in length and are usually sent by the personnel representative who interviewed the candidate. In addition, the sender should personalize the letter by signing it, and not leave this up to a clerk or secretary to do. Finally, rejection letters should begin and end on a positive note. The sample letter shown in Figure 4 encompasses these points.

SUMMARY

This chapter discussed the components of the final selection process. Guidelines for conducting effective reference checks were offered. Three different types of references were then analyzed: employment, educational, and personal. Both written and phone references were reviewed, and suggestions for checking with an applicant's present employer were offered as well.

In addition to information regarding references, the other factors to be considered before making a final selection were provided. A discussion of who should make the actual hiring decision followed. Finally, methods of notifying the chosen candidate, as well as those not selected, were discussed.

8

Orientation of New Employees

To many employers, the term *orientation* means sending new employees to a two-hour briefing about the company's history rules, and benefits. While these are certainly important elements of an individual's introduction to his or her new work environment, they are not likely to be understood comprehensively in just a few hours, nor do they tell the whole story. A comprehensive orientation program for new employees consists of three different stages: the new employee's first day of work; a formal organizational orientation program; and a departmental orientation program.

Careful preparation for each stage will ensure more effective and productive employer–employee relations.

THE FIRST DAY OF WORK

As soon as a prospective employee's starting date is confirmed, his or her supervisor or manager should make a notation to keep that day as free of appointments as possible. This way, full attention may be given to meeting the needs of the new worker. If a clear calendar cannot be arranged, then at least some time during the day—preferably, first thing in the morning—should be set aside to spend with the new employee. Arrangements should also be made for someone else (e.g., another supervisor or manager from within the department) to assist the new employee in getting settled.

Introductory Remarks

When the new employee reports to work for the first time, devote several minutes to putting him or her at ease and establishing rapport. To accomplish this, employ the same techniques used during the interview process, including ice-breaker questions and statements. Consider the following examples.

> "I'm sorry we couldn't arrange better weather for your first day of work; the weather report predicts that the rain should stop early this afternoon, however."
>
> "We at XYZ, Inc., try to think of everything. We even arranged a beautiful, sunny day for your first day of work!"
>
> "I'll bet the construction on the expressway cost you about 15 minutes this morning. Before you leave today, I'll have someone give you directions for an alternate route."
>
> "You're lucky you didn't start here two weeks ago when the transit workers were on strike; commuting then was a nightmare."
>
> "Were you able to locate your assigned parking space without much difficulty?"

Be careful that your initial ice-breaker statements do not make the new employee feel unduly pressured. For instance, a greeting such as, "Thank goodness you're finally here! The work on your desk is already a mile high!" could make the employee wonder if he or she made a mistake in accepting your job offer. All you want to do at this stage is to calm first-day jitters and make the individual feel comfortable.

Following your ice-breaker remarks, take a few moments to describe the scheduled activities of the day. If a great deal has been planned, then a typed agenda might be appropriate. Otherwise, briefly describe what is to occur. To illustrate:

> Janet, after we finish talking, I'll take you around the department to meet everyone. Then, I'm going to turn you over to Bruce Jenkins, our Production Manager. He'll show you your office, tell you where everything is, and essentially explain how to get around. I'll meet you back here at 11:45 so we can go to lunch.

I've made reservations for us at the officers' dining room. The food there is quite good. Then, at 1:30, Bruce will take you over to the Human Resource Department for the first part of the organizational orientation program. When that ends at 4:30, come back to my office so we can talk. I'll answer any questions you may have formed throughout the day, and we can discuss what's been scheduled for tomorrow.

Before moving on from this step in the employee's first day of work, be sure to tell the person how you wish to be addressed. This may not seen terribly important to you, but to a nervous employee who wants to make a good impression, it can result in some awkward moments. Simply say:

By the way, we're very casual around here, so please call me Phyllis. Everyone is on a first-name basis except when you get to the executive vice presidents' level and above: they like things a bit more formal; in fact, they'll address you as Ms. Bower. The only time they relax on this is at the annual picnic. I guess when they're playing softball and eating hot dogs, they feel it's okay to use first names.

The introductory remarks described thus far take only a few minutes to accomplish, yet they contribute a great deal to a new employee's perception about the company. These perceptions will affect the employee's attitudes towards his or her job, which, in turn, will affect productivity. Therefore, care should be taken to be as encouraging, supportive, and sincere as possible.

Introductions

Now it is time to introduce the new worker to others with whom he or she will be working. Generally, these individuals will all be in the same department. Sometimes, however, introductions extend to employees in other units. This may occur when the new person will be working on a regular basis with other departments. If there are to be more than a half a dozen introductions, it is a good idea to have a sheet typed up in advance with everyone's name, title, office location or number, and telephone extension. This can help make the experience less overwhelming, since the new employee will have it to refer to after the introductions have been completed.

As you take the new employee around, be careful not to express your opinions about the other people. For example: "Janet, the next person you're going to meet is Bob Johnson. Watch out for him during staff meetings; he's notorious for stealing ideas and submitting them as his own." Or: "When I introduce you to Fred Waters, don't take it personally if he acts like he doesn't like you. He applied for your position through job posting, but was rejected. He thinks you cheated him out of a promotion."

Positive statements should be avoided as well. For example: "Janet, I'd like you to meet Rod Perret. Rod can always be counted on to help you meet impossible deadlines."

New employees should be permitted to form their own opinions about their co-workers. Therefore, any statement that is subjective or judgmental should be avoided. Instead, focus on being descriptive. As you approach the desk or office of each worker, briefly describe his or her overall function. Limit yourself to one or two sentences per person so that the new employee will later be able to remember what you said. Think in terms of action words, as described in Chapter 1. For instance, you might want to say, "The next person you will be meeting is Terry Carson. Terry is our Office Manager. She receives all the work to be typed from the department's assistant vice presidents, distributes it among the secretaries, reviews the final product, and then returns it to the appropriate A.V.P." Therefore, if the new hire were making notes, he or she could quickly write, "Terry Carson: Office Manager: Receives, distributes, and returns typing to A.V.P.s."

Familiarization with the Office

Once the introductions have been completed it is time to show the employee exactly where he or she will be working, and to explain where everything is located. Generally, a sponsor will be assigned to the new person for this purpose. Be certain that the person selected is thoroughly familiar with the office layout and can devote the amount of time necessary to explain everything.

Preparation for this stage of the new employee's first day of work should include a checklist of items to make certain that no details are omitted. This list might include the following points.

1. *Show the employee his or her office or desk.* It is likely that this is the first time the individual will be seeing exactly where he or she will be working. If the employee is to be situated at a desk in close proximity to other workers, explain what the others do in relation to his or her responsibilities. If the employee has a private office, describe any company policies pertaining to pictures on the walls, plants, or other personal touches. Some organizations are rather inflexible about such matters, and employees should be so informed at the outset.

The desks of all new employees should be filled with necessary supplies (e.g., pencils, pens, pads, staplers, rulers, letter openers, paper clips, rubber bands, tape and scissors). Additional equipment, such as calculators, computers, typewriters, word processors, or dictaphone machines, should also be provided, as appropriate. Relevant reference materials, such as a dictionary and a thesaurus, should also be available.

2. *Show the employee where supplies are located and/or explain how to order supplies.* Describe departmental procedures regarding additional supplies. It may be that there is a central supply room and employees merely go there and take whatever they need. If this is the case, take the employee to the room and briefly explain where everything is located. If your organization requires employees to fill our requisition forms for additional supplies, explain where to get the forms, who to give them to when completed, and approximately how long it takes to receive the requested items. Also explain any exceptions to the regular policies. For example, ordering a new chair or desk will undoubtedly require more paperwork, and probably more signatures, than requesting a pair of scissors.

3. *Provide the employee with a telephone directory.* All employees should know how they can reach others within the organization. A directory of departments, key employees with corresponding titles, and telephone exchanges should be provided.

4. *Explain how the phone system works.* Many organizations now have rather complex phone systems. It is rare that one can

simply pick up a telephone and dial the desired number. Therefore, be certain to thoroughly explain the use of such factors as prefixes, special codes, intercom systems, outside lines, transferring calls, holding calls, and conference calls.

5. *Show the employee the location of restrooms and water fountains.* It is amazing how many employees hesitate to ask about the location of these two items. It only takes a moment to tell the new employee where the restrooms and water fountains are located. If there are several throughout the department, point them out.

6. *Explain the time and location of the coffee wagon.* Everyone wants to know how and when they can get coffee, danish, and the like. If your organization has a food wagon that comes around to each department, tell the new hire approximately what time he or she can expect it each day, and exactly where it stops. You might also include any information you have as to what is offered and a sample of prices.

7. *Show the employee the location of photocopy machines and explain how they are used.* Most departments have at least one photocopy machine. Show the employee where it is located and explain any required procedures for its use. In some companies all duplicating is done by a clerk. If this is the case, indicate who is in charge of this task, and where he or she is located. In other organizations, everyone does their own photocopying. In this event, demonstrate how the machine is operated. Be certain to demonstrate procedures for multiple copies, enlargements or reductions, colored copy and collating. Also, explain how paper is to be changed and who to contact if the machine malfunctions.

8. *Show the employee the location of files.* Show the new person where the department's files are located and explain how they are set up. Also describe any procedure for signing out a file.

9. *Show the employee the cafeteria and/or executive dining room.* Take the new employee on a brief tour of the cafeteria. Describe what kind of food is generally offered and the price range. Also provide the hours it is open. If by virtue of his or her title, the employee is entitled to eat in the executive dining room, include this in your tour as well. Be sure to provide information re-

garding its hours, reservations if required, method of payment, and policy pertaining to guests.

10. *Show the employee the location of the employee lounge.* If your organization has an employee lounge, take the employee on a brief tour of it. Describe which activities are permitted there, and which are prohibited, (e.g., eating, smoking, watching television, playing the radio, or playing games).

11. *Explain the use of company cars.* An employee whose work requires traveling from one organizational location to another is often provided with a company car. If this is the case, explain who the employee should contact for details regarding this matter.

12. *Show the employee any exercise facilities.* More and more companies are reflecting the times by providing their employees with an exercise facility. This may include a running track, gymnastic equipment, and even group exercise classes scheduled before and after working hours. If your organization has such a program, be certain to describe eligibility for and frequency of use, required gear (e.g., sneakers), and hours.

13. *Explain procedures for medical care.* Explain the procedure that is to be followed in the event that an employee requires nonemergency medical care, including any forms to be filled out, and where to go.

14. *Show the employee any child care facilities.* If your organization has a child care program, take the new employee on a brief tour and explain how it operates. Be sure to include eligibility requirements, a description of who watches the children, how many children are assigned to each caretaker, and the cost. Provide the employee with the name of who to contact for additional information.

It is a good idea to give a list highlighting the 14 categories just described to the new employee so that he or she can jot down notes as you talk. A sample of a checklist for new employees appears in Appendix J. If possible, also provide the employee with a floor plan.

It is important to note that some of the points already mentioned (e.g., seeing the cafeteria, employee lounge, exercise facility, and child care facility) may also be included in a tour conducted as part of the organizational orientation. At this stage, repetition can only serve to reinforce what the employee is being told and shown.

Taking the New Employee to Lunch

By the time the lunch hour rolls around on a new employee's first day of work he or she is probably feeling somewhat overwhelmed. Therefore, arrangements should be made for someone to take the person to lunch. This is usually done by either the employee's immediate boss, or the sponsor who has been in charge of showing the person around. Sometimes, a new employee's co-workers assume this responsibility. In any event, it should be someone who, in all likelihood, will be eating with this person again in the near future.

If your company has a cafeteria, it is a good idea to go there, so that the individual can begin to become familiar with its offerings. In addition, informal introductions to other employees who are in the cafeteria at that time can be made while eating. If the person is an exempt employee, then plan on eating in the executive dining room.

Remember that your purpose in taking a new employee to lunch is to make the person feel welcome and comfortable. Be careful that you do not get carried away, as did the executive who insisted on taking a new clerk in his department to the executive dining room for lunch. His intentions were good, but the gesture was inappropriate. The clerk, quite understandably, enjoyed the experience immensely, and fully expected it to be repeated. It was his very first job and he did not realize that the meal he had just had in the executive dining room was an exception to normal procedure. He waited for the vice president to invite him again, and when the invitation was not forthcoming he began to assume that there was a problem with his job performance. Eventually, his work was affected, and his six-month performance review reflected satisfactory work, as opposed to outstanding work.

The End of the Day

It is strongly recommended that new employees attend orientation for at least part of the first day. If this cannot be arranged, then the balance of the day should be devoted to introducing the employee to departmental policies and procedures in some other fashion. A full discussion of departmental orientation appears later in this chapter.

Regardless of how the day is spent, it should conclude the way it began: with a meeting between the new employee and his or her supervisor or manager. A period of approximately 30 minutes should be set aside to discuss what took place during the day and to answer any questions the employee may have. In addition, the following day's agenda should be reviewed.

ORGANIZATIONAL ORIENTATION

Virtually all organizations have some sort of orientation program for new employees. Unfortunately, many employers hesitate to invest more than a minimal amount of energy, money, or staff time in this critical stage of a new employee's career. Indeed, some consider it a waste of valuable time—time that could be better spent working. This kind of thinking can have a detrimental effect on both employee performance and attitude and, in turn, result in disciplinary problems and increased turnover. Taking the time to acclimate the new worker to his or her company can have the opposite effect. The employee is more likely to form positive impressions and consequently care more about the quality of his or her work.

The Purpose of Orientation

A well-planned organizational orientation program is designed to help new employees feel welcome and knowledgeable about their new organization. More specifically, it will:

Give new employees an overview of the organization's history and present status
Describe the company's overall functions
Explain the organizational structure

Describe the organization's philosophy, goals, and objectives

Explain how vital each employee is in helping to achieve company goals

Describe the benefits and employee services offered

Outline the company's standards of performance, rules, regulations, policies, and procedures

Outline safety and security practices

Naturally, the exact information provided and the amount of time required for an orientation program will vary with each organization. In a small company, for example, a one-day session will probably be adequate. In very large corporations, a full week is frequently devoted to orientation. Follow-up sessions several weeks or months later are also quite common. Regardless of the duration of your program, it is critical that the ingredients already outlined be included, and that representatives from human resource and other key departments partake in the presentation of information. Detailed information regarding the content of an organizational orientation program will follow later in this chapter.

Participants

As already stated, all new employees should be required to attend the organizational orientation program. In some companies, new employees in all job classifications participate in the same program. In other companies, one presentation is offered to exempt employees and another is provided for nonexempt employees. This is frequently done for two reasons: first, there are too many new employees for a single program; and second, there is a substantial difference in the specific information offered (e.g., managerial benefits and policies pertaining to executives may differ). In smaller companies everyone generally attends the same session, regardless of their title.

While orientation programs are designed with the new employee in mind, inviting existing employees to attend should also be considered. A refresher on such matters as corporate goals and standards of performance can be very helpful to *all* employees. It can also help motivate existing employees by making them feel that they are still important to the company. Having these individuals attend the same session as new employees may be effective, since it allows for an exchange between the newcomers and the existing workers. Usually, however, a separate session is scheduled in order to avoid unnecessary repetition of certain points and to keep discussions on a more advanced level.

Because discussion is an important element of an effective orientation program, the number of participants should be limited to a maximum of 20. The ideal group size is from 12 to 15. This encourages an exchange between the new employees and still allows for questions to be asked and responded to. Having less than 6 employees can make the participants feel conspicuous and self-conscious.

Location and Setting

The site selected for your organizational orientation program should be centrally located and convenient for most employees to reach. It should easily accommodate the number of people scheduled to attend, but should not be too large. Tables should be provided, since literature is likely to be distributed and because employees will probably want to jot down notes during the course of the presentation. Tables and chairs should be arranged in a casual manner; round tables are preferred over tables and chairs arranged classroom style. For these reasons, auditoriums should be avoided.

Content

As noted earlier, there are eight main areas to be covered in an orientation program. These may be expanded to encompass several additional components. Depending on the size and complexity of your organization, the following topics may be considered for inclusion in your orientation program.

History
Present status
Philosophy, goals, and
  objectives
Structure
General expectations of
  all employees
Overall function
General industry
  information and
  special terminology
Unique organizational
  features
EEO and affirmative
  action policies
Rules and regulations
Probationary period
Standards of
  performance
Grading system
Performance review
  process

Salary increase
  guidelines
Pay day
Training and
  development
Growth opportunities
Job posting
Promotions
Transfers
Insurance
Vacation
Holidays
Personal days
Sick days
Tuition reimbursement
Employee club
Pension plan
Savings incentive plan
Safety and security
  practices

Generally speaking, an orientation program should emphasize what employees can expect to receive from the organization and what the organization expects to receive from them. In addition, orientation should expose employees to the larger picture of the overall function, status, structure, philosophy, and goals of the organization. It is believed that this holistic view can benefit individuals in their present jobs, help them develop a sense of commitment to the organization, and help them plan a future with the company.

Departmental Representation

The next area to consider when planning orientation is departmental representation. That is, who should conduct and/or be actively involved with the program. Three different groups should be considered: (1) representatives from human resources;

(2) experts in each topic; and (3) officers from major departments.

It is generally agreed that someone from human resources should be in charge of the overall program. This entails:

Planning the content
Scheduling the speakers
Preparing the presentation media and supplemental material
Reserving space
Scheduling employees
Making opening and closing remarks
Introducing each speaker
Conducting tours

Because of this wide range of responsibilities, the human resource representatives selected should be knowledgeable about the organization and should have presentation skills. The latter is important if enthusiasm and interest is to be generated among the participants. Also, to keep orientation leaders from going stale, a rotational system is recommended, so that no one person conducts orientation every time it is offered.

Experts in various topics should also be involved. For example:

1. A benefits expert might discuss insurance, the pension plan, and the savings incentive plan.
2. A salary administrator might discuss the grading system, the performance review process, and salary increase guidelines.
3. A member of the Training and Development Department might discuss growth opportunities and tuition reimbursement.

As with the human resource representative, these topical experts should be knowledgeable and should possess group dynamic skills. Particularly with dry subjects, such as insurance, it is critical that the presenters are able to facilitate interest and retention.

Finally, all employees, regardless of classification, should be familiar with key organizational officers. Having representatives from senior management participate in the orientation program will accomplish this end. In addition to welcoming new people into the organization, officers might briefly describe the primary functions of their respective departments and discuss how their units relate to the organization as a whole. This will add to the employee's holistic view of the company. Furthermore, minority and female representatives from senior management may serve to promote an organization's EEO and affirmative action policy and inspire future growth.

Format

Orientation information can be imparted in a variety of different ways. In fact, variety is considered essential to the success of a program where a great deal of new information is going to be presented.

There are several different formats from which to choose.

Lecture by one or more speakers
Transparencies and/or charts
Handout materials
Films and/or slides
Question and answer periods
Tours

As previously discussed, having representatives from several different departments participate in orientation is highly desirable. However, regardless of how interesting these individuals may be, a straight lecture format is discouraged. Supplemental transparencies and/or charts highlighting key points will help employees understand and retain what is being presented. Providing handout materials illustrating what has been said is also recommended. Use of professionally-prepared films and/or slides can be very effective as well. The primary objection to using a film, as opposed to slides, is that updating a film is far more difficult and expensive than revising slides. In addition, questions raised during the course of a film have to wait until it is over in order to be addressed.

Answering questions as soon as they occur is far more preferable than having a formal question and answer period. Encouraging a free exchange between speakers and participants promotes a more relaxed, less intimidating atmosphere.

A tour of major company departments is also recommended. This will enable employees to more fully understand how their work relates to the work performed in other units of the organization.

Timing

As was mentioned earlier, employees should be encouraged to attend orientation as soon after beginning work as possible. Indeed, some organizations require new employees to attend before their first day on the job. This is not recommended, since most people continue to work for another employer until beginning a new position. Taking time off to attend an orientation program is usually quite impractical.

The first day of work is usually the best time to begin orientation. Employees are not yet caught up in the details of their jobs, and there is little chance of receiving inaccurate information from other sources. More specifically, the afternoon of the first day is considered ideal. As described earlier in this chapter, the first morning should be devoted to departmental introductions and office familiarization. Once new employees have had the opportunity to become somewhat acclimated to their new environment they are ready for more detailed information about the organization.

Duration

As previously stated, the exact duration of an orientation program will largely depend on the size and complexity of your organization. In relatively small companies a minimum of one day is recommended; in very large corporations, a full week or more is usually needed to cover all of the key points.

One alternative that is growing in popularity is the flexible mode orientation program, whereby a general session during the first few days of employment is followed by detailed modules of varying duration in subsequent weeks and months. This method provides employees with basic information at the very beginning of their employment, and then provides them with more specific information after they have had an opportunity to become more familiar with their work and surroundings. This progression from general to detailed information also ensures greater retention. The only real drawback to this kind of scheduling is the potential for conflict with departmental deadlines. However, advance notification of session scheduling and cooperation on the part of department heads should preclude any problems of this nature.

SAMPLE ORIENTATION PROGRAM

Following is an example of an organizational orientation program, which may be modified to meet the needs of your particular environment. It has been designed for a fictitious medium-size bank, Future Savings, and is patterned after the flexible mode concept. It consists of four separate segments: (1) general session; (2) tour; (3) detailed benefits session; and (4) detailed policies and procedures session.

Segment 1: General Session

This segment will provide new employees with a comprehensive view of employment at Future Savings Bank. In general, it will encompass three principal areas: (1) an overview of the banking industry in general, and Future Savings in particular; (2) a synopsis of what Future Savings offers its employees; and (3) a summary of what the bank expects from its employees.

More specifically, the first area—an overview of banking and Future Savings—should cover:

1. A brief description of the banking industry: what it entails, how it compares with other financial businesses, and what makes one bank more successful than another. It is suggested that reference be made to the fact that a bank's long term, overall success depends on how effectively it utilizes its human resources.

2. A short summary of the history of Future Savings, citing its origins, tracing its growth, noting its major accomplishments, and describing its present status in the banking community.

3. A description of the bank's philosophy, present status, and objectives.

4. General, frequently-used banking terminology. The sooner employees adapt to their new work environment, the sooner they will be able to concentrate on their specific job responsibilities. Familiarity with the unique language of banking will facilitate this adjustment.

5. An overview of the bank's structure and hierarchy. A broad picture of Future Savings and a look at the composition of its major departments (e.g., banking operations, fiduciary, and metropolitan banking) should provide the new employee with an idea of the size and organization of the bank.

6. General information regarding the interrelationship between various departments and functions.

7. Statements regarding the bank's EEO and affirmative action policies. It should be clearly explained that the bank's policy pertains to every aspect of an individual's relationship with Future Savings, including recruitment, selection, compensation, benefits, training and development, educational tuition, social and recreational programs, promotions, transfers, relocation, discipline, termination, and all other privileges, terms, and conditions of employment.

The next area to be covered in the first orientation session should be a summary of all the benefits that employees may expect. Because the bank offers so much in the way of benefits, and since there are so many other topics that should also be discussed during this first session, it is recommended that the following benefits merely be mentioned and described very briefly at this point in the program.

Vacation
Holidays
Personal days
Sick days
Pay day

Training and development opportunities
Tuition reimbursement
Employees' club
Special bank services

All of these benefits should be described in greater detail in a subsequent orientation session. The purpose at this time is to merely make the employee aware of all the programs available to those working at Future Savings.

Because employees are eligible for insurance coverage immediately upon hire, an in-depth discussion of the following is recommended.

Life insurance
Medical and disability insurance
Travel accident insurance
Pension plan
Savings incentive plan

The third main area to be mentioned at this first overview session concerns what Future Savings expects of its employees. Once again, the intent here is to familiarize; a more intense session pertaining to rules and policies will follow shortly.

In this regard the following Future Savings policies and procedures should be mentioned.

Overall expectations of Future Savings employees
Grading system
Importance of customer service
Job posting
Performance review process
Probation period
Promotions
Rules regarding such matters as attendance and punctuality
Salary increase guidelines
Standards of performance
Transfers
Safety and security practices

If effectively presented, this general session will accomplish a number of objectives. To begin with, new employees should leave an introductory orientation session with a positive overview of their work environment. At Future Savings this means pointing out all the advantages of working for a bank in general, and the advantages of working at Future Savings in particular. There may be a number of reasons why someone accepts a job at future Savings, ranging from needing a job, to wanting to work for a financial institution, to specifically wanting to work for Future Savings because of its reputation. Being able to assume the latter would be wonderful, but rather unrealistic. It is far safer to assume that most new employees know very little about banking and even less about Future Savings. Therefore, orientation is the bank's opportunity to explain all the attributes of banking and particularly the advantages of working at Future Savings. The reason for doing this is, quite simply, a matter of improving motivation and, thus, productivity. (According to the classical and widely accepted motivational theories of Maslow, McGregor, Herzberg, Ouchi, and others, there is a direct correlation between employee motivation and productivity.) If the bank accepts this relationship as one that is not only valid, but quite effective, then this general orientation program provides the ideal arena for initially creating a highly-motivating environment.

To reiterate, one of the goals of this general session is to have new employees leave feeling motivated and inspired about working at Future Savings. This should lead employees to: become actively involved with their specific job duties and responsibilities; become an integral part of Future Savings; and plan a long term future with Future Savings.

Part of the process of making the bank attractive to new employees involves describing all of the benefits that Future Savings offers its staff. The time to boast of all these extras is immediately, reiterating the general benefits outlined during the interviewing process and talking about some others at length.

Inspiring new employees to plan a future at Future Savings, based on a highly motivating environment and available benefits, is a critical aspect of the general orientation session. Equally important, however, is a clearly-outlined description of expected employee performance. Employees need to understand at the outset that Future Savings operates on a system of exchange: the advantages of working for the bank are given in exchange for abiding by its policies and rules.

Therefore, another purpose of this first session is to provide new employees with an accurate picture of what working at Future Savings entails, vis-a-vis its overall expectations. It is absolutely critical that all new employees be told immediately upon hire just what the bank requires of them. If this data is clearly and consistently disseminated at the outset, numerous negative performance-related incidents may be avoided. For example, managers and supervisors may assume that employees realize that they should call in when they are not coming to work. However, an employee may previously have worked for someone who did not require this or may have no previous work experience and, therefore, not be aware of this requirement.

It is unfair to assume that any employee—regardless of where they may have worked in the past—knows anything regarding the specific policies of a new employer. If the rules are not spelled out in the very beginning, it is conceivable that there may be incidents in subsequent months that could adversely affect that person's chances for growth within the bank. These occurrences can easily be avoided by telling new employees what is expected of them at the very beginning.

The key to successfully disseminating new information lies in creating an environment that is conducive to learning, and presenting the data in a manner that is both interesting and varied. Based on this, the following is recommended.

1. Create a casual, relatively unstructured environment (e.g., a round table, as opposed to tables and chairs arranged in classroom style).

2. Allow orientation participants to gather over refreshments before the actual session begins. This should help people relax and briefly get to know one another. By the time the session begins, names will have been exchanged and there will not be any unfamiliar faces.

3. Introduce the banking industry and general information about Future Savings, using a short film or slides. Using the visual media to accompany anything historical or statistical should not only make the subject more interesting, but should also help to reinforce the accompanying verbal messages.

4. Distribute a glossary of frequently-used banking terminology.

5. Utilize transparencies and charts to highlight the bank's structure and hierarchy.

6. Utilize slides to illustrate the interrelationships between various departments and functions.

7. Incorporate the verbal statements of a human resource representative concerning the bank's EEO and affirmative action policies.

8. Have a presentation by a Future Savings benefits expert about the various insurance plans available. Slides, charts, and transparencies may also be used for this segment. This presentation should be followed by small group discussions relating to the information provided by the benefits experts, so that employees will fully understand their options before completing any of the required insurance cards. The benefits representative could spend a few minutes sitting with each group to clarify any points about which employees have questions.

9. Briefly describe all other Future Savings benefits.

10. Distribute a booklet highlighting the main topics covered and a directory of names, titles, and telephone numbers of people to call with questions relating to the topics described or discussed.

11. Distribute the employee handbook.

This general orientation session should run for a total of one whole day. It may begin after lunch on an employee's first day of work and then be continued on the following morning. The overnight break will allow employees to digest what has been said thus far, thereby preventing the feeling of being overwhelmed by new material.

Segment 2: Tour

Following the general session, employees should be taken on a tour of the bank's major departments and one typical branch. Seeing a department in action will serve to supplement the information provided in the general session. Arrangements should be made in advance for representatives of each department to guide the employees through the department, explaining how it operates. If specific departmental literature is available, it may be distributed at this time.

In addition to a tour of key bank departments, employees should be shown such places as the:

Employee cafeteria and/or executive dining room
Employee lounge
Exercise facilities
Medical unit
Child care facilities

The hours, functions, and any eligibility requirements of each unit should be described.

It may be that new employees have already been taken on a tour of these places by their department heads. If this is the case, a second trip will contribute to an employee's feelings of familiarization with his or her new environment.

The tour segment should begin on the afternoon of an employee's second day of work and be continued on the morning of the third day.

Segment 3: Detailed Benefits Session

This session will provide detailed information regarding all of the bank's employee benefits. Since an overview of all employee benefits will be mentioned briefly during the general orientation session and all areas of insurance will be covered in detail, this session will elaborate on other, noninsurance benefits. It will include:

1. *Vacation.* Details might include eligibility, formula for calculation, and unique stipulations pertaining to holiday add-ons or leaves of absence.
2. *Holidays.* Details might include eligibility, specific dates, any unique stipulations pertaining to absences the day before or after a holiday, and adding holidays onto vacations or leaves of absence.
3. *Personal days.* Details might include eligibility, number of days allowed, purpose, and required procedure.

4. *Sick days.* Details might include eligibility, number of days permitted, uses, and required procedure.
5. *Pay day.* Details might include frequency, method, check cashing, advances, and pay day occurring during vacations or leaves of absence.
6. *Training and development opportunities.* Details might include programs available, enrollment procedure, eligibility, frequency, and correlation with career planning.
7. *Tuition reimbursement.* Details might include eligibility, types of courses, grade requirements, registration fees, books, maximum number of courses or credits, and procedure.
8. *Employee club.* Details might include its purpose, what it offers, how events are publicized, and who to contact for detailed information.
9. *Special bank services.* Details might include eligibility and required approval for free checking, travelers checks, safe deposit boxes, installment loans, and advanced checking.

A detailed benefits session will serve two primary purposes: it will show employees that the bank is concerned about their immediate needs and future development, and it will ensure a consistent application of all available benefits to new employees.

Using a variety of training media is recommended in order to ensure a clear understanding of the information presented in this segment. This might include: lectures by human resource representatives, followed by discussion; slide presentations; transparencies and charts; and handout materials.

To foster a comfortable learning session that encourages open communication and questions, an informal seating arrangement and possibly refreshments are recommended.

It is recommended that this benefits orientation session run for one half-day. This amount of time should be sufficient, since some benefits will be reviewed in the general session. In addition, if literature is distributed to new employees when they first report to work, it will enable them to prepare for this in-depth session.

This benefits session will be most effective if conducted one week after the general session. At that time, an elaboration of the specific benefits should serve to reinforce and clarify the information presented during the first couple of days.

Segment 4: Detailed Policies and Procedures Session

This session will provide detailed information regarding the bank's policies and procedures. Because an overview will be presented in the first general session, this more detailed session will elaborate and more specifically explain the bank's policies relevant to all employees. It will include the following topics.

1. *Grading system.* Details might include purpose, and correlation with salary.
2. *Customer service.* Details might include why it is important, who it affects, and possible ramifications of poor customer service.
3. *Job posting.* Details might include purpose, eligibility, types of jobs posted, how long jobs are posted, requirements, and procedure.
4. *Performance review process.* Details might include purpose, frequency, measurement factors, correlation with standards of performance, and salary increases.
5. *Probation.* Details might include purpose, duration, and extension.
6. *Promotions.* Details might include eligibility requirements, procedures, correlation with grading system, and salary increase guidelines.
7. *Rules regarding such matters as attendance and punctuality.* Details might include importance, possible ramifications of poor attendance and/or punctuality, requirements, and procedure.
8. *Salary increase guidelines.* Details might include procedure, eligibility, frequency, correlation with performance review process, and standards of performance.
9. *Standards of performance.* Details might include purpose, measurement factors, correlation with performance review process, and salary increases.
10. *Transfers.* Details might include eligibility, voluntary

and involuntary transfers, procedures, correlation with grading system, and salary increase guidelines.

11. *Safety and security practices.* Details might include procedure and guidelines.

A session on policies and procedures that supplements literature describing the bank's requirements and explains the reasons behind some of the rules will set the tone for greater compliance. If an institution expects its employees to obey certain rules and regulations, it has an obligation to provide full and detailed information about these rules and an open exchange to assure clear understanding. Therefore, every opportunity should be provided for employees to ask questions.

To create an environment conducive to learning, a relaxed format is recommended. As already mentioned, an informal seating arrangement and the offer of refreshments might be considered. Varied media will contribute to heightened attention levels and retention of information disseminated. Media might include: slide presentations; lectures by human resource representatives, followed by discussion; transparencies and charts; and handout materials.

This policies and procedures session should run for one half-day. This should allow sufficient time to cover the important policies that apply to everyone. As with employee benefits, an overview of policies and procedures will have been presented in the general session and literature will have been presented in advance.

This policies and procedures session should take place two weeks after hiring (one week following the benefits session). By this time, employees will have adjusted somewhat to the new work environment and will therefore be in a better position to understand why certain policies and rules exist, as well as how they apply.

DEPARTMENTAL ORIENTATION

In addition to the topics covered on the employee's first day and during the organizational orientation, there are other areas with which a new employee should be familiar. These topics are most effectively covered during an orientation session conducted within the employee's own department. The person conducting this orientation should be the same person who helped the new employee become acclimated on the first day of work. A rapport with this person will have already been established, thereby making the employee feel more comfortable.

Content

Departmental orientation should focus on specific job-related areas. Following are some topics considered relevant for inclusion.

1. *Departmental responsibilities.* Details might include its origins, overall function, and both long term and short term goals.
2. *Department structure.* Details might include the identification of specific functions and the incumbents in specific positions.
3. *Disciplinary procedure.* Details might include an outline of the general disciplinary procedure, sample infractions, and ramifications of same.
4. *Grievance procedure.* Details might include steps to follow, people to contact, time frames, and examples of legitimate grievances.
5. *Hours of work.* Details might include starting and quitting times, and flex-time eligibility and options.
6. *Interrelationship between own department and other departments.* Details might include a description of the flow of work between departments and the key individuals to contact in other departments.
7. *Job duties and responsibilities.* Details might include a description of exact tasks to be performed, expected frequency of performance, areas of responsibility, and interrelationship with other jobs, both within the department and with other departments.
8. *Meal and break periods.* Details might include how meal and break periods are scheduled and frequency and duration of breaks.

9. *Meal money.* Details might include eligibility for meal money, maximum amount, and procedure.
10. *Overtime.* Details might include requirements, eligibility, frequency, and scheduling.
11. *Personal telephone calls.* Details might include under what circumstances personal telephone calls are permitted.
12. *Personal visitors.* Details might include where personal visitors may be met, and I.D. requirements.
13. *Reporting relationships.* Details might include direct and indirect reporting relationships, and who is in charge during absences of the people normally in charge.
14. *Smoking regulations.* Details might include both restrictions and areas where smoking is permitted.
15. *Time records.* Details might include sign-in sheets, and records of sick days, vacation days, and personal days.
16. *Vacation scheduling.* Details might include how vacations are scheduled, who approves vacation requests, and how far in advance requests should be made.

It is advisable to have a topical checklist of these categories, similar to the one used on the employee's first day of work, in order to make certain that nothing is omitted. Giving a copy to the new employee so that he or she can take notes as you talk is also advised.

Materials Used

If the new employee will be working in a supervisory or managerial capacity, be certain to provide him or her with a copy of the organization's policies and procedures manual. Take time to familiarize the individual with the overall content, explaining how and when the manual is to be used. Also be certain to mention the person who should be contacted if clarification is needed.

If deemed appropriate, also provide the new employee with a departmental table of organization. Go over it with the employee, describing the primary functions of each position and individual as you do so.

In addition, provide the employee with work manuals, instructions, or other printed materials relative to his or her specific job.

Timing

It is recommended that this departmental orientation take place on the afternoon of the employee's third day on the job, if at all possible. Having by this time received a general introduction to his or her environment, it is fitting that he or she receive full departmental information before actually beginning to work.

SUMMARY

This chapter has provided information relative to three different aspects of orientation for new employees: the first day of work, organizational orientation, and departmental orientation. Important components of each aspect of orientation were described and recommendations were made regarding such matters as timing, duration, and format. In addition, a sample organizational orientation program was provided, consisting of four distinct segments: a general session, a tour, a detailed benefits session, and a detailed policies and procedures session.

The following orientation schedule has been recommended.

Day 1: A.M. — Familiarization with the office.
P.M. — Organizational Orientation, Segment 1: General Session.
Day 2: A.M. — Organizational Orientation, Segment 1: General Session (Conclusion).
P.M. — Organizational Orientation, Segment 2: Tour.
Day 3: A.M. — Organizational Orientation, Segment 2: Tour (Conclusion).
P.M. — Departmental Orientation.

Week 2: One half-day—Organizational Orientation, Segment 3: Detailed Benefits Session.

Week 3: One half-day—Organizational Orientation, Segment 4: Detailed Policies and Procedures Session.

Readers are urged to modify the model program and schedules to suit the needs of their particular environment.

Appendix A:
Job Description Form

Job Description

Job Title:

Division/Department:

Reporting relationship:

Location of job: Work schedule:

Exemption status: Grade/Salary range:

Summary of duties and responsibilities:

Primary duties and responsibilities:

1.

2.

3.

4.

5.

6.

7.

8.

9.

Performs other related duties and assignments as required.

Job title:

Division/Department:

*Education, prior work experience, and specialized skill
and knowledge:*

Physical environment/working conditions:

Equipment/machinery used:

Other (e.g., customer contact or access to confidential information):

Job analyst:
Date:

Appendix B:
Job Posting Notice Form

Job Posting Notice

Job Title:
Division/Department:
Location: Job no.:
Summary of primary duties and responsibilities:
Exemption status: Grade/Salary range:
Work schedule/Working conditions:
Qualifications/Requirements:

                                   Closing date:

Job Posting Eligibility Requirements:

1. You must be employed by XYZ, Inc. for at least 12 consecutive months.
2. You must be in your present position for a minimum of 6 months.
3. You must meet the qualifications/requirements listed above.
4. Your most recent evaluation must reflect your job performance as satisfactory or better.
5. You must notify your immediate supervisor/manager of your intent to submit a job posting application.

Job Posting Application Procedure:

1. Complete a job posting application form, available in the Human Resource Department.
2. Return the completed form to the Human Resource Department and give a copy to your immediate supervisor/manager by the closing date noted above.
3. You will be contacted within three working days of receipt of your application.

Appendix C:
Job Posting Application Form

Job Posting Application

(Please print or type)

Date:
Name: Telephone ext.:

Present job title: Present div./dept.:

Present grade: Present salary:

Name of present supervisor/manager:

Position applied for: Job no.:

Job Posting Eligibility Requirements:

1. You must be employed by XYZ, Inc. for at least 12 consecutive months.
2. You must be in your present position for a minimum of 6 months.
3. You must meet the qualifications/requirements listed on the job posting notice for this position.
4. Your most recent evaluation must reflect your job performance as satisfactory or better.
5. You must notify your immediate supervisor/manager of your intent to submit a job posting application.

Job Posting Application Procedure:

1. Submit the original copy of this form to the Human Resource Department; submit the yellow copy to your immediate supervisor/manager; keep the white copy for yourself.
2. You will be contacted within three working days of receipt of your application.

© Copyright 1985 by Arthur Associates Management Consultants, Ltd., Garden City, N.Y.

Appendix D:
Sampling of Job Ads

Although job ads will vary in terms of content, all ads should contain certain key elements. This includes information about the company, and specific job requirements and responsibilities. In addition, a statement regarding benefits and compensation should be offered, as well as contact information. Reference to being an equal opportunity employer should be made as well. Of course, the overall appearance should be eye-catching and easy to read. Following is a sampling of six ads, illustrating varying degrees of effectiveness.

Job Ad Sample Number 1

personnel

SALES TRAINER

The sales training programs of the Miller Brewing Company are among the most sophisticated of their kind, and are part of the reason our products are so visible in the competitive brewing industry. This is your opportunity to align your training and development talents with these outstanding programs, at our headquarters in Milwaukee.

You will be responsible for developing and implementing sales training programs for Miller distributors and retail clients. You will also advise sales management on employee training and development techniques. Approximately 30% travel is involved.

Previous classroom sales training/development experience is required as is bilingual (Spanish & English) abilities; a degree is preferred. As an operating company of a Fortune 50 corporation, Miller Brewing Company can provide you with a competitive salary and complete fringe benefits. For confidential consideration send your resume or letter of qualification to: Ken Deakman, Dept. 9000-85, MILLER BREWING COMPANY, 3939 W. Highland Blvd., Milwaukee, WI 53201. **Employing and promoting Equally today and tomorrow.**

MILLER BREWING COMPANY ®

Overall appearance: Logo identifies company, attracts reader's attention, and builds company image. Use of white space effectively isolates subtopics. Graphics are simple and effective.

Job title: Clearly stated.

Information about the company: Effectively linked directly with the job opening.

Job specifications: Duties and requirements are clearly explained.

Contact information: Provides information regarding who to contact; offers option of resume or letter of qualification.

Benefits and compensation: Stated in minimal terms.

EEO information: Uniquely stated.

Source: Training and Development Journal, March 1985

Job Ad Sample Number 2

EDP Instruction

Technical Education Specialists

Don't miss this opportunity to learn about NCR. You'll discover the high corporate priority we place on the education of our customer service representatives. NCR knows where it's going in field engineering training, as we develop the very finest training programs ever created for field service engineers.

Now you can help lead the way. Your development efforts will include Self Paced, Computer-Based Training and instructor-taught courses for both hardware and software. The programs you generate here will not only be comprehensive, but will redefine the state-of-the-art in EDP instruction.

And your career will be backed by our $3.7 billion enterprise . . . highly successful in every segment of information processing. With a host of new product innovations, keen marketing insight, and a new spirit of enthusiasm, NCR looks forward to a high growth future ahead . . . for us and for you.

Right now, we have immediate openings in our expanding Technical Education Organization for instructors and course developers experienced in the training of field engineers. You must have a Bachelor's Degree, or equivalent; comprehensive knowledge of the design and implementation of Criterion Referenced Instruction; and the willingness to relocate to Dayton, Ohio. Involves some travel assignments.

We offer excellent compensation, extensive benefits, advancement potential and the opportunity to contribute significantly to our dynamic organization.

Our doors are open. Send your resume with salary history to: Mr. Keith Jenkins, NCR Corporation, U.S. Data Processing Group, Dept. L-339, Dayton, Ohio 45479

NCR
1884-1984
Celebrating the future

An **equal** opportunity employer

Overall appearance: Professional in design, but too cramped. Variation in size and boldness of print would make content easier to read.

Job title: Clearly stated.

Information about the company: Detailed information regarding company's priorities and the field itself are designed to motivate readers.

Job specifications: Responsibilities and requirements are adequately explained but difficult to isolate. Subheadings would help reader identify different topics.

Contact information: Provides information regarding who to contact.

Benefits and compensation: Concisely stated.

EEO information: Readers are informed that the company is an Equal opportunity employer.

Source: Training and Development Journal, November 1984

Job Ad Sample Number 3

Experienced professional need to direct multifaceted training activities in expanding retail organization. This is a hands-on position and requires exceptional interpersonal and presentation skills, must have proven ability to create and implement new and effective programs using the ranges of state-of-the arts communication techniques. The highly organized and effective administrator who has a minimum of four years experience and is degreed in behavorial science, communications or business will be rewarded with great opportunities for creativity, recognition and growth. The compensation package which includes a full array of benefits is highly competitive. Write in confidence to Box 203.

Personnel Administrator
606 N. Washington Street, Alexandria, VA 22314

Overall appearance: Stark; single paragraph and lack of variation in size and boldness of print makes content difficult to read.

Job title: Unclear.

Information about the company: Virtually nonexistent.

Job specifications: Requirements range from being vague ("effective administrator") to restrictive ("four years experience and is degreed in behaviorial science, communications or business"); responsibilities not clear.

Contact information: Blind ad.

Benefits and compensation: Stated in minimal terms.

EEO information: Not mentioned.

Source: Personnel Administrator, June 1985

Job Ad Sample Number 4

TRAINING MANAGER
FINANCIAL SERVICES

Our aggressive, industry-leading financial services firm is seeking an experienced training professional for the corporate headquarters training team. The ideal candidate will be an assertive decision maker capable of administering consumer related training programs to complement the corporation's new marketing directions and product lines. This is a real opportunity for someone who has the ability to perform and the potential to grow. Bachelor's degree (MBA a plus) and a minimum of 5 years corporate training experience required. Good verbal/written communication skills are mandatory.

Reporting to the Assistant Vice President of Personnel, your responsibilities will encompass:

- **Design, production, implementation of branch and headquarters training programs for all employee levels.**
- **Evaluation, revision and update of current programs.**
- **Influencing the skill level of remote locations in an OJT mode.**

We offer a comprehensive and competitive benefits package including full graduate level tuition support, and a salary commensurate with experience. Candidates should forward resume and salary history, in strictest confidence, to: Personnel Director, Beneficial Management Corporation, 200 Beneficial Center, Peapack, New Jersey 07977. Equal Opportunity Employer M/F/H.

Beneficial

Source: Training and Development Journal, December 1984

Overall appearance: Use of figures is eye-catching and reflects company's awareness of affirmative action by using one white male, one female, and one minority; use of white space makes the ad easy to read; position responsibilities set apart in bold print is effective.

Job title: Clearly stated.

Information about the company: Virtually nonexistent.

Job specifications: Requirements include two extremes of very general, ("ability to perform") to very rigid ("Bachelor's Degree . . . and a minimum of 5 years corporate training experience"); key responsibilities clearly stated, using action words.

Contact information: Information regarding who to contact and what information to forward is clearly stated.

Benefits and compensation: Information regarding tuition support is eye-catching.

EEO information: Addition of "M/F/H" is effective.

Job Ad Sample Number 5

INDEPENDENT MARKETING REPS

We need additional marketing representatives to follow-up on leads, as well as to develop their own clients. Part-time or full-time.

We are the best known organization in North America for the measurable results we achieve in writing courses using our guided study formats and personal tutor-counselors.

Excellent commissions and repeat business provide the basis for a "growth enterprise of your own.

EDUCATIONAL ENTERPRISES OF NEW YORK
90 Dayton Avenue
Manorville, NY 11949

Overall appearance: Use of white space makes ad easy to read.

Job title: Clearly stated.

Information about the company: Stated in simple and concise terms.

Job specifications: No requirements listed; job responsibilities stated in very general terms.

Contact information: No mention of what to submit or who to contact.

Benefits and compensation: Vague language.

EEO information: Not mentioned.

Source: Training and Development Journal, March 1985

Job Ad Sample Number 6

PERSONNEL DIRECTOR

Methodist Health Services, Inc. a multicorporation organization is seeking a highly qualified individual to assume responsibility for the Personnel Department. Responsibilities cover Methodist Hospital, a 225-bed acute care hospital, Methodist Health Center, a 120-bed nursing home, Methodist Retirement Center, a 210-unit apartment facility for independent older adults. This position has responsibility for planning, directing, coordinating and controlling the personnel policies and practices of these various facilities.

The individual we seek will have a bachelor's degree in personnel, employee relations or a related business program. A master's degree in personnel or business administration is preferred. Three to five years' of previous personnel management experience demonstrating a working knowledge of compensation, benefits administration, staffing and recruitment, employee relations and relevant legal issues is required.

Madison, Wisconsin offers a unique living environment with many recreational, educational and cultural activities. The University of Wisconsin offers opportunities for continuing education and interaction with the academic community. Interested persons should send their resumes and salary history in confidence to: **Yvonne Evers, Employment Manager, Methodist Health Services, Inc., 309 W. Washington Ave., Madison, WI 53703, or call (608) 258-3250.** We are an equal opportunity employer.

METHODIST HEALTH SERVICES, INC.

Source: Personnel Journal, May 1985. Reprinted courtesy of Methodist Health Services, Inc., Personnel Department.

Overall appearance: Use of logo, graphics, and varying size and boldness of print attracts readers' attention. Use of white space makes contents easy to read.

Job title: Clearly stated.

Information about the company: Minimally stated.

Job specifications: Range of responsibilities clearly explained; use of action words highlights primary duties; requirements effectively described, but restrictive in terms of degree and number of years experience.

Contact information: Provides information regarding who to contact and specific information required.

Benefits and compensation: Unique approach: no mention of salary or health benefits—instead, description of location and educational and cultural benefits.

EEO information: Readers are informed that the company is an equal opportunity employer.

Appendix E:
Application for Employment Form

Application for Employment

(Please Print)

XYZ, Inc. considers applicants for all positions without regard to race, color, religion, sex, national origin, age, veteran
status, or non-job-related handicap.

Date: _____

Name: _____
          last   first   middle

Address: _____
            number   street   city   state   zip code

Phone no.: (___) _____ Social security no.: _____
            area code

Position(s) applied for: _____

Available to work: (   ) Full time   (   ) Part time
                     (   ) Days   (   ) Evenings

Referral source: (   ) Advertisement (   ) Employment agency
                   (   ) Friend   (   ) Relative   (   ) Other

Have you ever filed an application at XYZ, Inc. before?
                  (   ) Yes   Date: _____   (   ) No

Have you ever been employed by XYZ, Inc. before?
                  (   ) Yes   Dates: _____   (   ) No

Do you have any relatives, other than a spouse, already
     employed by XYZ, Inc.? (   ) Yes (   ) No
     If yes, please list names: _____

Are you above the minimum working age of _____ and below
     the mandatory retirement age of _____?
                              (   ) Yes (   ) No

Are you a U.S. Citizen: (   ) Yes (   ) No
   If not, do you possess an alien registration card?
                                (   ) Yes (   ) No
   If yes, please provide your alien registration no.:
   _____

Have you ever been convicted of a felony? (   ) Yes (   ) No
   If yes, please explain: _____
   _____
   _____
   _____
   _____

Do you have any physical, mental, or medical impairments
   that would interfere with your ability to perform
   the job for which you are applying? (   ) Yes (   ) No
   If yes, please explain: _____
   _____
   _____
   _____
   _____

Have you ever served in any of the U.S. military services?
                                (   ) Yes (   ) No
   If yes, what branch? _____
   Briefly describe your duties:
   _____
   _____
   _____
   _____

What languages do you speak, read, and/or write?
   _____ (   )   (   )   (   )   Degree of
                 Speak   Read   Write   Fluency
                                           _____

   _____ (   )   (   )   (   )   Degree of
                 Speak   Read   Write   Fluency
                                           _____

   _____ (   )   (   )   (   )   Degree of
                 Speak   Read   Write   Fluency
                                           _____

What professional organizations or business activities
are you involved with, relative to your ability to
perform the job for which you are applying? _____

_____

_____

_____

_____

Employment Experience

Please list present or most recent employer first. If additional
space is needed, continue on a separate sheet of paper.

Employer: _____ Phone no.: (   )
                 area code

Address: _____
     number   street   city   state   zip code

Position(s): _____

Super./Mgr.: _____ Start. $: _____ Final $: _____

Dates employed: From: _____ To: _____
           mo. yr.   mo. yr.

Reason for leaving: _____

_____

Description of primary responsibilities: _____

_____

_____

_____

Employer: _____ Phone no.: (   )
                 area code

Address: _____
     number   street   city   state   zip code

Position(s): _____

Super./Mgr.: _____ Start. $: _____ Final $: _____

Dates employed: From: _____ To: _____
           mo. yr.   mo. yr.

Reason for leaving: _____

_____

Description of primary responsibilities: _____

_____

_____

_____

- -

Employer: _____ Phone no.: (   )_____
                                               area code

Address: _____
            number   street   city   state   zip code

Position(s): _____

Super./Mgr.: _____ Start. $: _____ Final $: _____

Dates employed: From: _____   To: _____
                              mo.   yr.   mo.   yr.

Reason for leaving: _____

_____

Description of primary responsibilities: _____

_____

_____

_____

- -

Employer: _____ Phone no.: (   )_____
                                               area code

Address: _____
            number   street   city   state   zip code

Position(s): _____

Super./Mgr.: _____ Start. $: _____ Final $: _____

Dates employed: From: _____   To: _____
                              mo.   yr.   mo.   yr.

Reason for leaving: _____

_____

Description of primary responsibilities: _____

_____

_____

_____

Education and Training

Type of School	Name and Location	No. Years Completed	Honors Received; Diploma/Degree	Course of Study
Elemen. School				
Jr. High/ High School				
Trade, Business or Technical				
College/ Univ.				
Graduate/ Profess.				
Other (explain)				

Please describe any additional academic achievements or relevant extracurricular activities: _____

_____

_____

_____

- -

Additional Qualifications
Please identify any additional knowledge, skills, qualifications, publications, or awards that will be helpful to us in considering your application for employment (include special office, technical, and clerical skills): _____

_____

_____

_____

References
Please provide the name, address, and phone number of three additional references, other than present/former employers:

1. _____

_____

2. _____

_____

3. _____

_____

_____

Special notice to disabled veterans, Vietnam era veterans, and individuals with handicaps
Government contractors are subject to Section 402 of the Vietnam Era Veterans Readjustment Act of 1974, which requires that they take affirmative action to employ and advance in employment qualified disabled veterans and veterans of the Vietnam era; and Section 503 of the Rehabilitation Act of 1973, as amended, which requires that they take affirmative action to employ and advance in employment qualified handicapped individuals.

If you consider yourself to be covered by one or both of these acts, and wish to be identified for the purposes of proper placement and appropriate accommodation, please sign below. Submission of this information is voluntary and failure to provide it will not jeopardize employment opportunities at XYZ, Inc. This information will be kept confidential.

( ) Handicapped   (   ) Disabled   (   ) Vietnam era
veteran   veteran

Signed _____

Agreement

I certify that the statements made in this application are correct and complete to the best of my knowledge.

I understand that false or misleading information may result in termination of employment.

I authorize XYZ, Inc. to conduct a reference check so that a hiring decision may be made. In the event that XYZ, Inc. is unable to verify any reference stated on this application, it is my responsibility to furnish the necessary documentation.

( ) You may   (   ) You may not contact my
present employer.

( ) You may   (   ) You may not contact the
schools I have attended for the release of my educational records.

If accepted for employment with XYZ, Inc., I agree to abide by all of its policies and procedures.

I also agree to have my photograph taken for identification purposes if hired.

Signed _____
Date _____

Do Not Write Below This Line

- -

Interviews

Human resource interviewer: _____Date: _____

Comments: _____

_____

_____

_____

_____

_____

Results: _____

Dept./Div. interviewer: _____Date: _____

Comments: _____

_____

_____

_____

_____

Results: _____

Dept./Div. interviewer: _____Date: _____

Comments: _____

_____

_____

_____

_____

Results: _____

Employed: (   ) Yes (   ) No

     If yes: Title _____

            Dept. _____

            Date of hire _____

            Starting salary _____

An equal opportunity employer M/F/V/H

Appendix F:
Completed Application for Employment Form

Application for Employment

(Please Print)

XYZ, Inc. considers applicants for all positions without re-   *Overall*
gard to race, color, religion, sex, national origin, age, veteran   *appearance:*
status, or non-job-related handicap.   *printed;*
                                                                          neat;

Date: **November 18, 1985**   *legible;*

Name: **Perkins   Valerie   Danielle**   *easy-to-*
       last   first   middle   *read*

Address: **23   Turner Avenue   Tyrone, N.Y. 65010**
     number   street   city   state   zip code

Phone no.: **(123) 614-2085**   Social security no.: **515-48-6234**
     area code

                      Assistant To The
Position(s) applied for: **Director of Human Resources**

Available to work: (**X**) Full time (   ) Part time
                  (**X**) Days   (   ) Evenings

Referral source: (**X**) Advertisement (   ) Employment agency
                (   ) Friend   (   ) Relative (   ) Other

Have you ever filed an application at XYZ, Inc. before?
            (   ) Yes   Date: _____   (**X**) No

Have you ever been employed by XYZ, Inc. before?
            (   ) Yes   Dates: _____   (**X**) No

Do you have any relatives, other than a spouse, already
   employed by XYZ, Inc.? (**X**) Yes (   ) No
   If yes, please list names: _____   *omission*

Are you above the minimum working age of __18__ and below
   the mandatory retirement age of __70__?
                  (**X**) Yes (   ) No

Are you a U.S. Citizen: (**X**) Yes (   ) No
   If not, do you possess an alien registration card?
                        (   ) Yes (   ) No
   If yes, please provide your alien registration no.:

Have you ever been convicted of a felony? (   ) Yes (**X**) No
   If yes, please explain: ———————————————————

Do you have any physical, mental, or medical impairments
   that would interfere with your ability to perform
   the job for which you are applying? (   ) Yes (**X**) No
   If yes, please explain: ———————————————

Have you ever served in any of the U.S. military services?
                    (   ) Yes (**X**) No
   If yes, what branch? ———————————————
   Briefly describe your duties:

What languages do you speak, read, and/or write?
  Spanish————(**X**) (**X**) (**X**) Degree of
               Speak   Read   Write   Fluency   *omission*

  French————(**X**) (**X**) (**X**) Degree of
               Speak   Read   Write   Fluency   *omission*

  ————————(   ) (   ) (   ) Degree of
               Speak   Read   Write   Fluency

What professional organizations or business activities
are you involved with, relative to your ability to
perform the job for which you are applying? **Member of**
Human Resource Development Specialists; Personnel
Specialists of America

Employment Experience

Please list present or most recent employer first. If additional
space is needed, continue on a separate sheet of paper.

Employer: **Q and R, ltd.** Phone no.: **(123) 518-4044**

area code

Address: **23-85   E. 36ᵀʰ St. Tyrone, N.Y. 65010**

number   street   city   state   zip code

Position(s): **Personnel Assistant** *starting*

Super./Mgr.: **Richard Simons** Start. $: **24,000** Final $: **27,500** *salary less*

Dates employed: From: **5 / 83**   To: **Present** *than final*

mo.   yr.   mo.   yr. *salary at*
previous

Reason for leaving: **No room for Advancement** *position*

gap of
7 months
Description of primary responsibilities: **Recruiting +** *between*
Interviewing; Reference Checks; Processing new *jobs*
hires; Assist with policies + procedures,
Salary admin. + performance appraisals;
EEO forms

- -

Employer: **Roxbury Medical Ctr.** Phone no.: **(712) 421-1900**

area code

Address: **2500   Oxford Blvd. Roxbury, Conn. 36401**

number   street   city   state   zip code

Position(s): **Personnel Assistant**

Super./Mgr.: **Eileen Cannali** Start. $: **24,500** Final $: **26,000**

Dates employed: From: **9 / 81**   To: **9 / 82**

mo.   yr.   mo.   yr. **"Red flag"**

Reason for leaving: **Personal**

Description of primary responsibilities: **Recruiting;**
Interviewing; references; processing new hires
benefits; orientation

- -

Employer: **Global Imports, Inc.** Phone no.: **(712) 469-2200**
area code
Address: **1725   Union Ave., Roxbury, Conn. 36401**   *Job title*
number   street   city   state   zip code   *requires*
Position(s): **Admin. Ass't.**   *explanation*
Super./Mgr.: **Jessica McDonald** Start. $: **21,000** Final $: **same**
Dates employed: From: **11 / 80**   To: **8 / 81**   *Pattern of*
mo.   yr.   mo.   yr.   *reasons for*
Reason for leaving: **No room for advancement**   *leaving*
                                                          starting to
                                                          emerge

Description of primary responsibilities: **Responsible**
for running the personnel dept.   *"Red flag"*

                                                          Frequency
                                                          of job
                                                          changes
- 9/81 - 9/82
                                                          11/80 - 8/81
Employer: **Vanderbilt Movers** Phone no.: **(123)**   1/80 - 12/80
area code   *omission*
Address: **1948   Tunney Blvd. Tyrone, N.Y. 65010**
number   street   city   state   zip code   *Job title*
Position(s): **Office Manager**   *requires*
Super./Mgr.: **Robert LaBlanca** Start. $: **16,000** Final $: **same** *explanation*
Dates employed: From: **1 / 80**   To: **12 / 80**   *Overlap*
mo.   yr.   mo.   yr.   *in dates*
Reason for leaving: **Conflicted with schedule at School** *between*
                                                          Vanderbilt
                                                          and Global
                                                          "Red flag"
Description of primary responsibilities: **Distributed work**
of 6 AVP's and VP's to Secretaries

Education and Training

Type of School	Name and Location	No. Years Completed	Honors Received; Diploma/Degree	Course of Study
Elemen. School	wilson Elem. School Roxbury, Conn.	6		general
Jr. High/ High School	Roxbury Jr. High and Roxbury High Roxbery, Conn.	6	H.S. Diploma	general
Trade, Business or Technical	N/A			
College/ Univ.	Roxbury Univ. Roxbury, Conn.	4	B.A. Degree	Sociology *Inconsistency between courses of study and employment*
Graduate/ Profess.	Tyrone Law School Tyrone, N.Y.	1½		Law
Other (explain)				

Please describe any additional academic achievements or relevant extracurricular activities: *French club; Spanish club; Debating Team (all at Roxbury U.)- Graduated with honors - 3.6 cum. index*

- -

Additional Qualifications

Please identify any additional knowledge, skills, qualifications, publications, or awards that will be helpful to us in considering your application for employment (include special office, technical, and clerical skills): *Excellent rapport with people*

References

Please provide the name, address, and phone number of three additional references, other than present/former employers:

1. **Jeff Brixton**   ?   **(712) 347-5591**   omission

2. **JoEL MEYERS   19 LODGE AVE. SAN CARLO, CALIF. 08070**   **(764) 223-0082**

3. **ROBERT LaBLANCA**   former employer
   **24 APPLE COURT DRIVE
   TYRONE, N.Y. 65010**   **(123) 942-3319**

Special notice to disabled veterans, Vietnam era veterans, and individuals with handicaps

Government contractors are subject to Section 402 of the Vietnam Era Veterans Readjustment Act of 1974, which requires that they take affirmative action to employ and advance in employment qualified disabled veterans and veterans of the Vietnam era; and Section 503 of the Rehabilitation Act of 1973, as amended, which requires that they take affirmative action to employ and advance in employment qualified handicapped individuals.

If you consider yourself to be covered by one or both of these acts, and wish to be identified for the purposes of proper placement and appropriate accommodation, please sign below. Submission of this information is voluntary and failure to provide it will not jeopardize employment opportunities at XYZ, Inc. This information will be kept confidential.

(   ) Handicapped   (   ) Disabled   (   ) Vietnam era
                                    veteran   veteran

Signed _____

Agreement

I certify that the statements made in this application are correct and complete to the best of my knowledge.

I understand that false or misleading information may result in termination of employment.

I authorize XYZ, Inc. to conduct a reference check so that a hiring decision may be made. In the event that XYZ, Inc. is unable to verify any reference stated on this application, it is my responsibility to furnish the necessary documentation.

(   ) You may   (**✗**) You may not contact my
                                     present employer.

(   ) You may   (   ) You may not contact the   *omission*
                                     schools I have attended for
                                     the release of my educational
                                     records.

If accepted for employment with XYZ, Inc., I agree to abide by all of its policies and procedures.

I also agree to have my photograph taken for identification purposes if hired.

Signed *Valerie D. Perkins*
Date *11/18/95*

Interviews

Human resource interviewer: _____Date: _____
Comments: _____
_____
_____
_____
_____
_____

Results: _____

Dept./Div. interviewer: _____Date: _____
Comments: _____
_____
_____
_____
_____

Results: _____

Dept./Div. interviewer: _____Date: _____
Comments: _____
_____
_____
_____
_____

Results: _____

<u>Employed:</u>   (   ) Yes (   ) No
      If yes: Title _____
            Dept. _____
            Date of hire _____
            Starting salary _____

An equal opportunity employer M/F/V/H

Appendix G:
Interview Evaluation form

Applicant Evaluation

Applicant: _____Date: _____
Position: _____
Department/Division: _____
Summary of experience: _____

_____

_____

Summary of education/academic achievements: _____

_____

_____

Relationship between position requirements and applicant's background, skills and qualifications:

Position Requirements	*Applicant's Qualifications*
_____	_____
_____	_____
_____	_____
_____	_____
_____	_____
_____	_____
_____	_____
_____	_____
_____	_____
_____	_____
_____	_____
_____	_____
_____	_____
_____	_____
_____	_____
_____	_____
_____	_____

Applicant: _____

Position: _____

Additional factors, as relevant:

    Clerical skills: _____

    _____

    _____

    Verbal communication skills: _____

    _____

    Writing skills: _____

    _____

    Technical skills: _____

    _____

    Numerical skills: _____

    _____

    Language skills: _____

    _____

Other job-related information: _____

_____

_____

Overall evaluation:
    (   ) Meets job requirements
    (   ) Fails to meet job requirements

Additional comments: _____

_____

_____

                      Interviewer: _____

Appendix H:
Employment Reference Form
for Exempt Positions

Exempt Employment Reference Check

Date:

- -

Applicant's name: _____   Position: _____
Person contacted: _____   Title: _____
Company: _____   Telephone no.: (   ) _____

Address: _____

- -

    The above named individual has applied to XYZ, Inc. for employment. He/She has listed you as a former employer, and has authorized us to conduct a reference check. We need your assistance in verifying and providing certain information regarding his/her work performance:

1. _____ worked in the _____
   department as a(n) _____
   from _____ to _____, and earned $_____
   at the time of termination.
   (   ) correct (   ) incorrect.
   If incorrect, please explain.

2. His/Her primary responsibilities included: _____
   _____
   _____
   _____

   (   ) correct (   ) incorrect.
   If incorrect, please explain.

Applicant's name: ——————— Position: ———————————
Person contacted: ——————— Company: ———————————
- -
3. He/She stated that his/her reason for terminating
   employment with your company was: ————————————

———————————————————————————————————————

   (   ) correct (   ) incorrect
   If incorrect, please explain.

4. How would you evaluate his/her overall work performance?

5. What were his/her greatest strengths?

6. What were the areas in which he/she required improvement
   and/or additional training?

7. What made him/her an effective supervisor/manager?

Applicant's name: ——————   Position: ——————————
Person contacted: ——————   Company: —————————
- -

8. How did he/she handle job-related situations involving pressure? Involving difficult tasks?

9. How would you describe his/her management style? Decision-making style?

10. Please provide an example of the type of decision he/she would commonly have to make on the job, and the ramifications of this decision.

11. How effectively did he/she handle meeting deadlines?

12. How did he/she generally respond to repetitious tasks? To new assignments?

Applicant's name: _____   Position: _____
Person contacted: _____   Company: _____
- -
13. Please describe any work-related travel required, in
    terms of location, duration and frequency.

14. This job calls for the ability to: _____.
    What experience did he/she have in doing this?
              (Note: This question can be expanded to
              encompass several different factors. Use
              your job description as a guide).

15. How effectively did he/she interact with peers?
    Senior management? Subordinates?

16. Would you rehire him/her?
    (   ) yes (   ) no
    If no, why not?

17. Is there anything else we should know about his/her
    work performance?

                         Reference conducted by: _____

Appendix I:
Employment Reference Form
for Nonexempt Positions

Nonexempt Employment Reference Check

Date:

- -

Applicant's name: _____   Position: _____
Person contacted: _____   Title: _____
Company: _____   Telephone no.: (   ) _____
Address: _____

- -

The above named individual has applied to XYZ, Inc. for
employment. He/She has listed you as a former employer, and has
authorized us to conduct a reference check. We need your assistance
in verifying and providing certain information regarding his/her
work performance:

1. _____ worked in the _____
   department as a(n) _____
   from _____ to _____, and earned $_____
   at the time of termination.
   (   ) correct (   ) incorrect.
   If incorrect, please explain.

2. His/Her primary responsibilities included: _____
   _____
   _____
   _____

   (   ) correct (   ) incorrect.
   If incorrect, please explain.

Applicant's name: —————— Position: ————————

Person contacted: —————— Company: ——————

- -

3. He/She stated that his/her reason for terminating
employment with your company was: ——————————

(   ) correct (   ) incorrect
If incorrect, please explain.

4. How would you describe his/her attendance record?
Punctuality record?

5. How would you evaluate his/her overall work performance?

6. What tasks did he/she perform particularly well?

7. What were the areas in which he/she required improvement
and/or additional training?

Applicant's name: _____ Position: _____
Person contacted: _____ Company: _____

- -

8. How closely did you need to supervise his/her work?

9. How did he/she respond to requests to work overtime?
   To be on call?

10. How did he/she respond to repetitious tasks?
    To new assignments?

11. How effectively did he/she interact with co-workers?
    With management?

12. This job calls for the ability to: _____.
    What experience did he/she have in doing this?

(Note: this question can be expanded to
encompass several different factors. Use
your job description as a guide).

Applicant's name: _____   Position: _____
Person contacted: _____   Company: _____
- -
13. Would you rehire him/her?
    (   ) yes (   ) no.
    If no, why not?

14. Is there anything else we should know about his/her
    work performance?

Reference conducted by _____

Appendix J:
Checklist for New Employees

1. Office/Desk
   a. Functions of other workers situated nearby
   b. Policies regarding pictures, plants, and other personal items
   c. Supplies:
      1. Pencils
      2. Pens
      3. Pads
      4. Staplers
      5. Rulers
      6. Letter openers
      7. Paper clips
      8. Rubber bands
      9. Tape
      10. Scissors
   d. Equipment:
      1. Calculator
      2. Computer
      3. Typewriter
      4. Word processor
      5. Dictaphone machine
   e. Reference materials:
      1. Dictionary
      2. Thesaurus
2. Supplies
   a. Location
   b. Procedure
   c. Exceptions
3. Telephone directory
4. Phone system
   a. Prefixes
   b. Special codes
   c. Intercom
   d. Outside numbers
   e. Hold
   f. Conference calls
5. Restrooms; Water fountains

6. Coffee wagon
   a. Time
   b. Location
   c. Offerings
   d. Cost
7. Photocopy machines
   a. Location
   b. Procedure for operation:
      1. Multiple copies
      2. Enlargements/reductions
      3. Colored copies
      4. Collating
   c. Changing paper
   d. Malfunction
8. Files
   a. Location
   b. Procedure for signing out files
9. Cafeteria/Executive dining room
   a. Location
   b. Food offered
   c. Cost
   d. Hours
   e. Reservations required (dining room)
   f. Method of payment (dining room)
   g. Guests (dining room)
10. Employee lounge
    a. Rules regarding its use
11. Company car
    a. Who to contact for additional information
12. Exercise Facilities
    a. Location
    b. Facilities offered
    c. Eligibility
    d. Hours
    e. Requirements for use
13. Nonemergency medical care
    a. Location
    b. Procedure

14. Child care facilities
    a. Location
    b. Eligibility
    c. Caretakers
    d. Cost
    e. Who to contact for additional information
15. Other

- -

Notes

INDEX